The Largest Theatre in the World

THE LARGEST THEATRE IN THE WORLD

THIRTY YEARS OF TELEVISION DRAMA

Shaun Sutton

British Broadcasting Corporation

For Ba

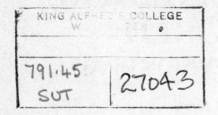
Published by the
British Broadcasting Corporation
35 Marylebone High Street
London W1M 4AA

ISBN 0 563 20011 1
First published 1982
© Shaun Sutton 1982

Set in 11pt Sabon 13pt leaded by
Input Typesetting Limited, London

Printed in England
by Mackays of Chatham

Contents

1	THE STORY SO FAR	7
2	STARTING POINTS	11
3	THE WRITER: THE SINGLE PLAY	15
4	THE WRITER: THE SERIES	30
5	THE WRITER: THE SERIAL	35
6	THE PRODUCER AND SCRIPT EDITOR	49
7	THE DIRECTOR: PREPARATION	66
8	THE DIRECTOR: LOCATION	88
9	THE DIRECTOR: REHEARSALS AND STUDIO	105
10	POST-PRODUCTION	121
11	THE RESPONSIBILITIES OF TELEVISION	128
12	WHAT NEXT?	139
	PICTURE CREDITS	154
	INDEX	155

1

The Story So Far

Television drama is an art in itself; no longer, as it was at first, a photographed stage play or a poor relation of the cinema film. It is itself, established and individual, with a maturity miraculously grown; an astonishing growth considering its short professional life. A young art – it made its debut in 1936 with a studio version of the stage success *Marigold* – its true potential was delayed by the war until the 1950s, when original television playwriting really began to blossom. Once that happened, its advance was assured and rapid.

There is nothing new about drama; its direct line has been unbroken for 2500 years beginning in the Greek amphitheatres with their masked actors and choruses, and progressing through Roman drama to the Middle Ages, when it was precariously maintained by miracle plays in cathedral closes and village booths. Then came the first formal playhouses of the Elizabethans, the exuberance of the Jacobeans, the jolly naughtiness of Restoration, the relative dullness of the eighteenth century (apart from Sheridan), through the unadventurous desert of the middle nineteenth century, until exciting drama exploded again with Shaw and Wilde and Ibsen and Pinero and a dozen more; a bonfire that, once lit, has blazed merrily ever since.

Britain has usually been rich in drama – we like it, we expect to see it. Today most large towns have their own theatres, even theatre complexes, and much of the work done there can rival that of the London theatre. Like most arts, theatre is woefully short of money, but this is probably no more than a phase in its very long life.

The heart of drama, its triple skills of writing, acting and direction and the emotions that inspire them, are surely the same today as they were for the Greeks and the Elizabethans. Shakespeare's company used the same craft as today's actors. Richard Burbage ran a successful repertory, and knew a good script when he saw it. These skills are ancient and unchanging. What does change is the outer shell of drama, its form and shape, its physical conventions. Each wave of young writers and directors dismisses the old way and discover a new one (or rather, rediscovers it, for there is nothing really new. What is the Olivier auditorium at the National Theatre but a Greek amphitheatre roofed in against the English weather?). It is a natural process, born of the energy of young writers and producers to whom the conventions of the preceding generation are always threadbare with use.

Television drama is no more than the newest presentation of an ancient art. It is, however, of a scope and size unequalled in drama history, with a fluidity denied to the theatre, an accessibility which outreaches the cinema. How amazed Shakespeare would be to learn that just one performance of his *Romeo and Juliet* had been watched simultaneously by an audience equal to the entire population of the England of his day; how quickly he would have adapted himself to the possibilities of the medium; how annoyed he would have been when *Titus Andronicus* was sent back to be rewritten.

There were three years of television before the Second World War closed it all down for the duration. There had been little enough drama, and what there was consisted of studio versions of stage plays (or just scenes from plays) with an occasional adaptation of the better-known classic to vary the diet. Throughout this period I can trace only four original drama scripts, one of which rejoiced in the title *The Underground Murder Mystery* and ran all of ten minutes.

Things were scarcely better in the immediate post-war years. The theatres were booming, and writers found in them plenty of scope for their work. The British film industry was vigorous, and regarded television drama with amused tolerance as an attempt to make crude instant movies.

Even the actors were wary of a medium that surrounded them with technical complications and afforded such infinite possibilities with which to make fools of themselves. Dark tales circulated of actors having to race the cameras from one set to the next, changing *en route* from dinner jacket to full armour. Television drama was all done 'live'. There was only one chance to get it right; no retakes, no second performances. If an actor 'dried', he did so unmistakably in full close-up with all the world and his agent as witness.

The directors of my generation all have disaster stories of 'live' television. My worst occurred in a wartime play, set in occupied France and bomb-scarred London. There was a sequence of scenes, cutting between a barn where the French Resistance planned their next coup, and a bombproof operations room deep below the War Office. For the barn scenes, I was unwise enough to include a brown cow and six chickens, to give an impression of bucolic reality. Throughout this tense scene, the chickens clucked gently, and the cow gave an occasional low moo. But no sooner had we cut to the bombproof operations room (in the adjacent set), with the dignified Chiefs of Staff around the table of destiny, than a fusillade of angry clucking broke out from the hens, and the cow loudly registered her boredom with television. The Staff Officers, trained actors to a man, continued their grave discussion unmoved by this farmyard commotion, fifty feet below London's pavements.

By today's elegant standards, studio equipment then was basic. The cameras were heavy and inflexible. Today's pedestal cameras can elevate and depress smoothly in vision; then one had to wait for a studio break or a rare cut to a film insert, and then crank the camera up noisily with a handle. John Glenister, today one of television's finest directors, was a studio cameraman with me in those early days. John is very tall, and I always asked him to go on to the pedestal camera, so that we automatically gained six inches of vertical height. Television lighting now challenges the best in feature film; it was considerably more all-purpose in the post-war years.

Sound was the studio Cinderella – the microphone had to force its way into the act after everything else had been settled.

The 'live' mode sorely restricted television writing. Scripts had to be tailored to allow cameras and actors time to move from set to set, for complicated costume or make-up changes. The pace was inexorable. Once the play 'faded-up', you kept going, even if the leading actor had a stroke half-way through.

Yet despite these limitations, in spite of the mis-cuts and mistakes, the camera 'shoot-offs' that revealed the entire studio in consternation; despite the microphone hovering always on the edge of frame and destruction, the drama itself had an extraordinary quality and energy. Perhaps it grew out of the inevitable tightrope feeling that came from 'live' TV; or perhaps it was yet one more example of the indestructible quality of actors, who delight in giving fine performances under the most difficult conditions. Nowadays the strains are different. Television drama is recorded in sections, and, if it goes wrong, there is always Take Two. But the route from the first glimmering of a dramatic idea to its realisation on the television screen is a long one. To take you along that route is the purpose of this book.

2
Starting Points

Television not only commands the largest drama audience in history – it offers it a rich variety of drama. A touch of a switch can produce Shaw, Shakespeare or Ibsen, or the three hundredth episode of the current soap opera. But there is a price for such rich fare. Television gobbles up ideas and innovations, digests them, exhausts them, and calls for more; the Arts are sometimes hard put to feed this voracity.

A good play in the West End may have a long life, and when that course is run, it repeats its success in regional and international productions. Films have multiple showings, endless repeats and, finally, a new life on television. But a television play uses up its potential in one night; it is seen, appreciated and, in a matter of days, probably forgotten because of the impetus of a dozen equally enjoyable programmes. It may, or may not, be given a repeat transmission a year or so later, and then either destroyed or lodged in some archive cellar. Between them, BBC and ITV need over a thousand drama scripts every year to fill the screens. Many might be rated routine or soap opera, but they are still dramas. Each has to be written, considered, rewritten, accepted, cast, rehearsed, directed, recorded and transmitted. Whether on location or in the studios, a standard series episode will engage much the same equipment or resources as a major play, the only difference being the actual time spent on the operation.

Relatively uncomplicated programmes abound in television – chat shows and quizzes, discussions on books and music, political confrontations, current affairs programmes. But there are no longer any simple dramas. Recording has brought its own technical excellence, eliminating error and crudity, ensuring better performances, subtler lighting and sound, more immaculate camerawork. But it has also opened the door to a host of new complications, and an increased army to cope with them.

Television drama starts modestly enough – a producer with his script editor seeking an idea and someone to write it. But once the script is secured, the cohorts gather. The play or episode must be planned into the television production line, given money and resources and space. It must be cast. It will be descended upon by experts – scenic, costume, make-up, graphic, lighting, sound and camera. If it includes filmed content, then locations must be found and crews arranged, accommodated and fed. Once in rehearsal, carpenters will build sets for it, painters will paint them, property men will prepare to fill them with furniture and dressing – everything from a fully edible Roman banquet to a space rocket. When the production arrives in the studio, a new army will take over – video cameramen, sound engineers, vision mixers, lighting crews, studio staff – this army will, in a matter of hours, convert the imagined backgrounds of the rehearsal room into 'reality'. The play, painfully rehearsed into one flowing piece, will be deliberately fragmented into scenes and shots, and recorded on tape by hidden engineers. Finally, it is reduced to a stack of tins containing tape which will be assembled by more experts – the tape editors. That done, a team of dubbing editors will give it the final overall polish, and the drama may then be pronounced fit for public consumption.

This army of experts is essential, because speed is the essence, time is literally money. Television drama in Britain is recorded faster than in any other country in the world, a rate of strike which derives from its very early days, when a studio was expected to rehearse and transmit thirty minutes of drama in one day.

Studio space is always at a premium, and the big television complexes use every device to streamline its use. As soon as a recording is complete, the studio is emptied of sets and properties, and a new show moved in, often overnight. The following day, the cycle begins again; sets are lit and dressed, cameras lined up, floors painted to look like cobbles or carpets or parquet, the names on the dressing-room doors changed. It is an operation of extraordinary efficiency, only noticed when it breaks down.

If ever there was a factory for the Arts, it is the television studio, with its ability to produce instant drama, opera, ballet, variety, chat shows and music. It is the home of the end product, the amalgam of the skills of writer, director, actor, designer and technician.

As in any drama medium, the weight of realisation falls on the director. Only he has the final concept in his head, from the first day with the script to the last day of rehearsal. In television he must carry an extra responsibility into the studio. He must know how to convert the images in his mind into pictures on the screen; if he is wise, he will have worked out beforehand what these images will be. Making it up as one goes along is a recipe for disaster. The television director works under urgent pressure. The rhythm of the theatre, with its try-outs and previews, allows time for more leisured decisions. The feature film, planned over long periods, can be concentrated on without distraction. Television is always up against a deadline.

The wise television director arrives at rehearsal with his intentions for the script and performances formed, plus at least a rough framework of the camerawork in relation to the settings. The drama must enter the studio artistically at boiling point, fixed in performance, so that it may survive the inevitable fragmenting of recording.

Certainly there are directors who are genuinely without a visual sense, who find it difficult to imagine the final pictures. Worse, by far, is the maverick, who, however brilliant, leaves the studio operation to chance. Staffs dread him, for he is a consummate time-waster, vacillating, using his actors as pawns in an irrelevant chess game, exhausting their tempers, and sometimes their performances, in the process; finally, inevitably running out of studio time. It is, I suppose, yet another tribute to the indestructibility of the actor that he can survive such a director's incompetence and still deliver an immaculate performance. In so technical a medium, a measure of homework is essential. The unprepared director will find himself overwhelmed by technique, bombarded by helpful suggestions from every corner of the gallery, diverted from the artistic demands of the play. Television drama is too complicated to do off the cuff. Preparation pays.

It pays with actors, who are grateful for efficiency. They welcome the director who marches into the rehearsal room and takes charge; who gives them mechanical moves that work and actually fit the lines they are struggling to say; who cuts and adds with authority, taking the technical weight and allowing them to develop their performances in a confident atmosphere. They particularly love the director who protects them in the studio, when the performances they have so painstakingly built up get chopped and recorded piecemeal. The achievement of a television drama is a drawn-out affair, a journey of many months.

But more of that later. Before it can begin at all, someone has to have an idea – and someone has to write it.

3
The Writer:
The Single Play

If television drama derives from centuries of theatre, the television play is its most legitimate descendant. Series and serials are recent, plays are antique. They generate from human mythology, from the sacrificing of goats (or people) on hilltops, stories told by the tribal chief or bard to the community. The play was probably born in the precarious climate of early civilisation, a sort of performed prayer, an appeal to the Gods for a bountiful harvest or heroic courage, as an investment against starvation or danger. After a few generations the tribe would begin to remember (or invent) its own heroes, by recalling their deeds in formal playlets. The more settled the community, the more likely they were to record their myths and the achievements of their heroes in terms of entertainment. The play-maker would become a privileged person, allowed to sit and stare. Continuity – the likelihood of one day succeeding another without catastrophe – is a condition that breeds the artist; amongst whom is the playwright.

Shakespeare and his contemporaries blossomed in just such a time of new security, in a society free at last from the civil strife of the Plantagenets, and the teething pains of the early Tudors. It was a time of national calm that allowed playwrights a liberality still not present today in the less fortunate countries of the world. No one told Shakespeare what he could or could not write; he was free to illuminate every corner of man's behaviour, with a sure magic we can only envy; and if he was careful not to offend his Tudor Queen with his portrait of her grandfather in *Richard III* that shows a cautiousness we can forgive. Is it too bold to suggest that today's television play descends directly from that golden age, through a roll-call of playwrights which includes Marlowe, Dryden, Webster, Jonson, Wycherley, Molière, Middleton, Goldsmith, Sheridan, Pinero, Wilde, Shaw, Ibsen, Brecht, O'Neill, Barker, Coward, Maugham . . .?

Yet, in spite of this illustrious ancestry, the television play is unique; at its best it combines the qualities of theatre and film, with a flexibility outreaching the first, and a domestic intimacy impossible for the second; a private playhouse for everyman, in the comfort of his home.

In post-war television, the arrival of the original play was long delayed. The directors came mostly from the theatre (not, as one might have expected from radio or the film world) bringing with them a repertoire of stage plays, which, for lack of anything else, they produced. Today, original television plays are taken for granted. But thirty years ago everyone was mesmerised by the new television toy; the sheer technical miracle of making instant films clouded all other issues. I doubt if it ever *occurred* to anyone, at first, to expect new plays – the established stage successes seemed very suitable; and the viewers, delighted with the new marvel, were not over-critical. Only a small percentage of the audience were regular thea-tregoers, and so many of them were actually seeing the great stage plays for the first time.

Other factors contributed. The post-war theatre was booming, and the repertory and the round-London theatres (in which I and many other later television directors worked) were the homes of the new playwright. This was their shop window; from here their plays often moved into the London theatres, bringing them income and reputation.

There were no fortunes to be made by television writers in those days. Transmissions were 'live' and there were no lucrative record-ings to be sold round the world. Writers had to be content with a modest once-for-all-plus-any-repeats fee. My own first radio and television scripts were paid at the rate of one guinea per minute (they paid by the clock) plus five guineas to underline the reckless generosity of the Corporation. These fees increased magically when commercial television arrived in 1955.

The amount of original drama between 1947 and 1950 was sparse, though it included some plays from Giles Cooper, Gerald Savory, Robert Barr and Frank Tilsey. The next five years were more cheer-ful, with writers like Alfred Shaughnessy, Roy Russell, John Whiting, Ian McCormick and Nigel Neale. Between 1955 and 1960 there were plays from William Fairchild, Elaine Morgan, John Mortimer, John Elliot, Tom Clarke, Rosemary Anne Sisson, Peter Nichols, Alun

Owen, Leo Lehman, Willis Hall, David Turner and John Hopkins. It was beginning to happen.

If there was a dramatic moment of truth for the single play, it was the early sixties. These were the years of the early David Mercer plays – *Where the Difference Begins, For Tea on Sunday, A Suitable Case for Treatment*. This was the time when the first play strands appeared – *Suspense, First Night, Studio Four, Festival*. The strand, or umbrella title, is often criticised as being a straitjacket for the writer, forcing him to distort his originality into a set format. That might be true of foolish strand titles like *Famous French Courtesans* or *Great British Bores*, paper-thin formulas emphasising nothing but the creator's lack of real talent. After the success of *The Six Wives of Henry VIII*, I was inundated by a deluge of facile follow-ups: *The Twelve Mistresses of the Roi Soleil, The Six Duchesses of Charles Stuart* – none of which, I am happy to say, ever got produced.

But a sensible strand title like *Playhouse* allows full scope to the writer, for its subjects are limitless, and it carries the bonus of a familiar weekly date with the viewer, an advantage much prized by television moguls, but also welcome to anyone looking for a larger audience. The strand also guarantees, as much as anything in drama can be guaranteed, an unbroken run of plays. For once it has been launched it has a juggernaut quality, not easily halted. The early strands were an extraordinary tonic to television drama, for they automatically guaranteed the presence of scores of new plays.

The year 1963 was a vintage one. It marked the arrival of the rumbustious Sydney Newman, who burst into the BBC Television Centre like a hurricane. Timing his entrance when television incomes were rocketing and the money flowing, he at once created a Drama Group out of a Drama Department, splitting the output into Plays, Series and Serials – and in the process making sure that each new arm of drama got a formidable increase in output. He established the all-the-year-round series on the American pattern; he put his stamp on the twice weekly soap opera. Most important of all, by his creation of a separate Plays Department, he underlined the importance of the single play.

Having established a score of long-running strands, he lost no time in inventing a new sort of television producer to look after them, each charged with the financial and artistic health of his particular strand of drama. The new producers were given independence and commanded to find new writers, new plays, new series; that done, they were to get the best directors to realise the scripts. At the same time Sydney pulled together all the major plays on BBC2 into one across-the-year strand, calling it *Theatre Six Two Five* after the higher 'line standard' of the second channel.

It wasn't long before he had done the same on BBC1, in doing so creating that most famous of all television strands – *The Wednesday Play*. This was Sydney's most personal, best loved baby, conceived out of his experience and success with *Armchair Theatre* at ABC Television but outstripping it in vision and quality.

It opened, most appropriately, with a Dennis Potter play called *Alice*, was soon followed by Nell Dunn's *Up The Junction*, Potter's two *Nigel Barton* plays, John Hopkin's *Horror of Darkness* and, a television landmark, Jeremy Sandford's *Cathy Come Home*. No play anywhere is better remembered than this moving story of a young married couple trying desperately to find a home. Some of its images – the burning caravan, the final terrible denouement at the railway station, when the children were forcibly taken from the young mother – will always haunt television drama makers. The strand has continued without interruption since then, though during the last decade it has been known as *Play for Today*.

Sydney galvanised television drama. He was brusque, sardonic and straightforward; stern when one made mistakes, fiercely supportive if anyone dared to suggest that you had. He was passionate about writers and writing, demanding new plays by the score. He was contemporary, irreverent, and a determined enemy of cant and pomposity.

He spread his enthusiasm through the group. Loud in praise, deafening in criticism, his language was robust. When he asked me to stop being a director and become his Head of Serials, Drama, his approach was unconventional: 'Shaun,' he said, 'they do a lot of these classic books in Serials. Have you read any of these classic books?' 'About three,' I said modestly. Sydney's reply was typical: 'I've only read two. Keep ahead of me.' All this was nonsense. We had both read classics by the score, but Sydney enjoyed being unexpected, and I enjoyed playing up to him.

There are no natural drama administrators; we are all shanghied into administration. I dreaded my first days in Serials. Sydney's advice was specific and comforting. 'Don't do anything Shaun. Just sit there and let it all happen. Don't make any decisions for six months. OK?' OK indeed. Six months was a lot of leeway. My first day in the department was full and intimidating, consisting of a series of visits from vastly experienced producers like Donald Wilson and Campbell Logan. They all greeted me warmly, at the same time politely indicating that they knew precisely what they were doing, and hoped that no one was thinking of altering anything. I was pondering this solid conservatism of the Serials producers, still bolstered by Sydney's last instruction to make no vital move for at least six months, when the telephone rang and irate tones filled the earpiece. 'Shaun,' he roared. 'When the hell are you going to start making decisions?'

I soon learned that this was Sydney's way of making sure that one was on one's toes. Actually, I didn't need the spur. I'd been on my toes since I was a sixteen-year-old stage manager in the theatre, earning my two pounds a week for a fourteen-hour day, seven days a week, under conditions that would horrify today's actors' union, Equity. But, on the whole, Sydney left his colleagues alone to cope with the huge mass of drama. He judged on results, and having bought himself a dog, he didn't bark himself. But he would make sporadic raids on your department, frightening everyone out of their wits by appearing suddenly in the corridors and demanding to know why we were all asleep on the job.

One of his passions was the BBC family science fiction programme, *Dr Who*, a unique serial he had part created. I don't think he would have greatly minded if I had rewritten *Oedipus Rex* and given it a happy ending but put a foot wrong with *Dr Who*, and the wires burned.

Sydney's accomplishment was the creation of a climate in which boldness paid. He wanted contemporary drama; he wanted to raise rumpuses and get questions asked. He wanted plays about drugs, bad housing, unmarried mothers, union struggles, students, unemployment, abortion, baby battering, wife beating. He spurned the long theatrical tradition that had locked plays into middle-class settings. He looked for plays about the underprivileged, the uneducated, the unemployed, the underdog.

Many of his writers were young anti-establishment, left-wing. Their plays were often one-sided, hectoring, unrelenting and lacking in humour. At their best they were disturbing and haunting, feeding one's sympathy and indignation, staying with one for days afterwards. Whatever else they were, they were not trivial.

There had been precedents for this type of play in the theatre. Ibsen's plays shocked his generation with their frankness. Shaw, in exquisite literary phrases, put the lower and middle classes under a microscope. But the theatre audiences to whom these plays were

directed were experienced playgoers, knowing what they were about
to receive. The impact of television is universal, sharp and personal,
and a play like *Cathy Come Home* can achieve an effect rarely
possible in the formal ambience of a theatre.

The late sixties were rich in good drama. John Hopkins wrote his
quartet of plays – *Talking to a Stranger*, David Mercer wrote *Let's
Murder Vivaldi* and *On The Eve of Publication*. There was *The
Gorge* by Peter Nichols, *The Big Flame* by Jim Allen, Nigel Kneale's
The Year of the Sex Olympics, Tom Clarke's *Mad Jack* and the play
sextet *The Six Wives of Henry VIII*.

So abundant were the seventies, I can only dip in at random and
bring out *Elizabeth R*, John Bowen's *Robin Redbreast*, Peter Ni-
chols' *Hearts and Flowers*. Ingmar Bergmann's *The Lie*, Jeremy
Sandford's *Edna the Inebriate Woman*, Tom Clarke's *Stocker's Cop-
per*, *The Wessex Tales*, Colin Welland's *Kisses at Fifty* and *Leeds
United*. There was Arthur Hopcraft's *The Reporters*, Dennis Potter's
Joe's Ark and *Blue Remembered Hills*, John McGrath's *The Cheviot,
The Stag, and the Black Black Oil*, Peter McDougall's *Just Another
Saturday*, David Hare's *Licking Hitler*, David Mercer's *Shooting the
Chandelier*, Trevor Griffiths' *Through the Night*, Frederick Ra-
phael's *The Glittering Prizes*, John Hopkins' *A Story to Frighten the
Children*, Hugh Whitemore's *84 Charing Cross Road*, Jack Rosen-
thal's *Spend Spend Spend*, Jim Allen's *The Spongers*, G. F. Newman's
Law and Order and *Billy*.

Were as many fine new plays produced in the London theatre in
this period? *The Wednesday Play/Play for Today* has never been
without its opponents: 'Must the plays always be so stark, so squalid,
so unsavoury?' 'Why do they always look on the dirty side of life?'
'Why are they always so left-wing/facist/perverted?' 'Why can't they
have a beginning, a middle and an end?' And in more magisterial
tones: 'Is this the proper use for the television play?' The simple
answer is that it is *one* proper use for the television play. There are
others – the classic, the lighter play, the thriller, even the old-
fashioned play with a beginning, middle and end. There is an audience for each, and each has its place. But if *Play for Today* disappeared overnight (and there are some who would light a candle to
the patron saint of propriety if it did) it would be mourned by more
than the professionals.

For those who would hasten its demise, there are practical arguments in plenty. The plays are costly, particularly when shot on film,
television's most expensive item. They usually draw small audiences

– if you can call four or five million small. Compared to the double figure millions of a popular series like *All Creatures Great and Small* it is certainly modest, but a play would have to run for decades in a theatre to be seen by so many. Nevertheless, the menacing graph showing high cost and low audience renders the television play vulnerable. Drama's administrators can, and do, argue that even a moderate viewing audience is acceptable providing the work is good; a long-held BBC principle. But television moguls are competitive creatures, ambitious for their output and reputations (though not necessarily in that order) and the single play will always have to fight for its place in the sun.

There are warnings enough. In the United States the pressures of network competition have all but eliminated serious plays, except the few that break out on the Public Broadcasting Service (of which more later). The national networks, CBS, NBC and ABC, may occasionally, as a flamboyant gesture, and provided the profit margin is safe, invest a few million dollars in a single 'special' of inordinate length; but anything of a challenging or disagreeable nature has less chance than a snowball in Hell.

In Britain, the single play holds on precariously, though it has had a rougher ride in independent television than with the BBC. It can certainly never relax and assume its automatic place in the schedules.

Britain is rich in television playwrights, richer by far than most European countries. I'm often asked what the rules are for writing a good television play. The answer is that anyone who can write a good play can write a good television play. A knowledge of camerawork or film cutting is not essential. Shakespeare, Shaw and Ibsen, indeed no playwright before the 1950s, had any such knowledge. Provided one has some sort of visual sense, the rules of television technique can be quickly learned. The sensitive writer will soon learn to build words and pictures together, to replace five lines of dialogue by a reaction close-up, a whole paragraph by a long shot. If the writer can see his scenes stand up before him as pictures, the rest follows. But technical knowledge is no substitute for writing talent.

Where do drama scripts come from? Who decides who shall write them, what they shall write about, and what to accept? The answer is that scripts can come from anywhere and anyone. Playwrights do not spring fully mature from the ground; they have to learn their craft. BBC Television alone receives thousands of unsolicited drama scripts every year, most of which are dealt with by a separate Script Unit. Out of these thousands, few are professional enough, or good enough, to merit acceptance and production. Playwriting is a special talent; were it not we would all be millionaires.

You cannot teach people to write, any more than you can make an actor perform beyond his talents, or a director beyond his. These skills are built-in, emotional, intuitive. If they are not present in the writer from the start, no amount of tuition can create them. You can tell a writer that his dialogue is limping, that his scenes do not build, that his points are not clearly made. You can note that the crisis of his play is too quickly, or too slowly, reached, that the characters of his leading man and woman keep changing improbably. But if the writer has not noticed this for himself, one is tempted to wonder how good he really is. What television can do, and does do, is to advise writers on the craft itself, on the alphabet of visual medium, the nuts and bolts that hold its scripts together.

There are few TV scripts at genius level – genius gets stretched thin in any art – but the overall standard of British television drama writing is highly professional. At one end of the scale there is a peak of excellent work, at the other a depression of bad scripts, though happily not too deep a depression. In the middle, there is a solid mass of professional scripts which work and please; and if the standard is sometimes marred by the bulk demands of the medium, that is the price one pays for so much drama.

It would be pleasant to record that a great part of this output comes from new writers, either by commission, or from unsolicited scripts. It would not be true. New writers are found every year, but most scripts are commissioned direct by the producer/script editor team – many from known and favourite sources; proven television writers, theatre dramatists, novelists, fringe playwrights. Today's television drama lacks nursery slopes for the new writer; it is all in the front line, and pilot productions are unknown. The more wonder that, one way and another, many new writers manage to achieve their first television production each year.

The search for new writers cannot be formalised in a phrase. It is not a job description. No one wakes up and says 'Today I will go out and find a new playwright of genius'. It happens unexpectedly in theatres and cinemas and offices, in chance conversations in canteens and clubs, a sudden recognition of something different and talented.

The end product is the same for everyone engaged in the making of a drama – the desire to hold and exhilarate an audience, to please them and disturb them, to challenge and delight them. To find a success, one that is not necessarily gauged by audience ratings but by its intrinsic quality.

Someone once said, about writing for the newspapers: 'It is well to remember that we are writing for an old lady in Hastings who has two cats, of which she is passionately fond. Unless our writing can sufficiently compete with her interest in those two cats, then it is no good'.

This is somewhat simplistic, for so much depends on whether our old lady is simple or sophisticated, prudish or permissive. But a grain of truth is there for the television writer, as for any other. A writer must find his own style. It must develop from within, personally and painfully; any attempt to impose it ends in imitation and parody. But one *can* help him by spelling out the limitations of television production, and this is part of the function of the script editor, working alongside the strand producer. A television studio can only hold so many sets; television budgets do not run to casts of hundreds; exterior filming must be kept within the allocated budget, and so on. Some writers find it hard to grasp that television drama is not in the feature film business, particularly such optimists as the writer who sent me the following:

SCENE: Night
A deep ravine spanned by a great railway viaduct. A passenger train approaches and begins to cross. The viaduct suddenly collapses and the train, with passengers falling from doors and shattered windows, crashes into roaring torrent at the bottom of the ravine.

The writer, perhaps suspecting that he was asking rather a lot, then added: 'Suggest use stock newsreel shot'. How fortunate that a newsreel cameraman happened to be crouched with his camera in the deep ravine on that particular night. How lucky he was that the train didn't fall on him!

One of the ironies of television is that the writers of the single play are often the least rewarded. Plays, often indigenous in subject and accent, do not sell abroad like series and serials. The single play writer may have to make do with a once-for-all payment, whilst the dramatiser of, say, *War and Peace*, will be receiving cheering cheques for years to come.

Television has always tended to straitjacket the length of plays; the sixty-minute play (fifty-two minutes on independent television, to allow for commercials) is popular with the scheduler. It is not ideal, indeed, no rigid lengths are ideal, for a play should be as long or short as it needs to be (though God defend us from too many four-and-a-half-hour epics!).

With the BBC Drama Group, I always strove for plays of all lengths, from the two-and-a-half-hour classic, down through ninety, seventy, sixty, fifty minutes, to the half-hour play. Seventy-five minutes is a useful length; it gives a play time to develop and resolve itself; and, to be practical, it does not overtax the tired viewer at the end of a difficult day at the office. Thirty-minute plays are neither easy to find or write; too often they emerge as dramatised short stories, with a neat little twist at the twenty-sixth minute; or, more often, as shapeless incidents, as if one had dropped in by accident into the middle of someone's life. They *can* be written as all-studio, or all-film (the *Première* series had some excellent examples of the latter) but they are a trap for the unwary writer who thinks they are trifles to be dashed off in an afternoon.

One of the bonuses of television is that it need not confine plays to single units. There can be trilogies, quartets, even six parters which are all in reality extended single plays. In 1965 John Hopkins' splendid dramatisation into a trilogy of plays of Ford Madox Ford's *Parade's End* was an early example; as was his later quartet *Talking to a Stranger*. In lighter vein there was *The Six Wives of Henry VIII*, and *Elizabeth R*. There was Dennis Potter's *Casanova*, *Sword of Honour* (based on the three Evelyn Waugh Second World War novels), the recent, and most moving, *The Lost Boys*, Andrew Birkin's study of J. M. Barrie, and the unique *Pennies from Heaven*. This startling original six-part play by Dennis Potter was a grim tale of seduction, prostitution, rape, murder and execution, set in the unemployed 1930s, when the loss of a job could mean near-starvation. This bleak story was punctuated throughout by the popular songs of the period; at any moment of truth, and scrupulously in line with the story, the characters would break into song to illustrate a point or a situation (unnoticed by the world around them) and then, as abruptly, return to reality and straight dialogue. It was an idea that could have foundered totally under the weight of its own audacity, but, in the event, brilliantly succeeded.

Drama Documentaries

This is a facile term wrongly applied to all sorts of television drama, mostly to modern plays with real or factual backgrounds. The better the play is done, the more believable, the more readily is the label applied, often with a hint of reproof, as if some sort of confidence trick were being played.

Thus, Tony Garnett's *Cathy Come Home* and *In Two Minds*, or his more recent *The Spongers*, are referred to repeatedly as drama documentaries, though in fact there was nothing of the *true* documentary about any of them. They were fictions, played by professional actors and actresses, including no portraits of real persons, alive or dead.

The distinguished string of Colin Morris/Gilchrist Calder social plays, starting in 1955 with *The Unloved* and leading to *Who Me?* in 1959 are officially recorded as documentaries, simply on grounds of content. There have been scores of such plays over the years – plays about homelessness, the mentally distressed, drunkenness, divorce, abandoned children, battered wives – subjects often meticulously researched against real cases, and filmed against authentic backgrounds; many of them deliberately cast with little known actors, to give a greater illusion of reality. But illusion it was, like all drama. It is a genre of drama that rouses controversy and misgiving. Television critics worry over the dividing line between fact and fiction; the doubts transfer themselves to the viewers, who begin to question the validity of what they have been watching. 'Were those real miners trapped underground?' they ask. 'Was that an actual headmaster in the school scene?' 'Were those real nurses in the hospital?' The merest suspicion in this area seems to rouse a curious apprehension that something not quite honest is going on; for which reason alone, it is important that the productions should be clearly labelled as what they are – drama.

Even with these positive identifications, plays can still fall foul of public misunderstanding. Although the *Play for Today* opening titles clearly preceded it, G. F. Newman's harsh quartet of plays, *Law and Order*, caused a deep anger in police and prison service circles. Yet these were fictions, invented and acted out. But because they dealt so realistically with a whole gallery of unsavoury characters – a cocky criminal arrested on false charges, a bribe-taking police officer, a shabby lawyer, and incompetent judge, brutal prison officers – they were criticised as if they had been real documentaries.

Pure documentary can be readily defined. It is the serious examination of a subject, a situation, a profession, an incident, a crime, an achievement. To achieve this, it will use real facts, words actually spoken or written, judgements taken and conclusions reached, plus expert opinions. If the documentary wishes to speculate, it must be equable in its speculation, reflecting all views. If an incident is re-created by actors, this must be plainly marked as a simulation. No true documentary will ever deliberately add or omit facts to further its argument.

It is not so simple in the fictional, emotional world of drama, particularly when one tries to separate the 'documentary drama' sheep from the 'dramatised documentary' goat. *The Search for the Nile, The Fight Against Slavery, The Voyage of Charles Darwin* were all made by the official documentary department of BBC Tele-vision. Yet all three were dramatically scripted and performed by actors. What did that make them – drama documentaries, or drama-tised documentaries? What was *The Naked Civil Servant*, the Thames television play about Quentin Crisp? Or *Spend Spend Spend*, the story of the huge pools win that marred the life of Vivienne Nicholson?

There are plenty more in this allegedly twilight drama world – *Suez, Churchill and the Generals, Speed King, Burgess, Philby and Maclean* and, most recently, *On Giant's Shoulders*, the story of a thalidomide child, who actually appeared in the play.

In most of these plays the characters were real people, living or recently dead, and the speeches spoken by the actors were often those which had been spoken in real life. They were plays written against factual backgrounds, well researched, but, ultimately, drama, coloured and augmented by the actors' performances.

It is true, if not particularly helpful, to add that the further you go back into history, the less likely you are to have a serious con-troversy. No one knows what Henry VIII said to Anne Boleyn when he proposed, but only the driest academic will be offended if the writer invents a pretty speech in good Tudor vein.

The difficulties begin when you enter the period of living memory and experience. Winston Churchill was revered by many, reviled by others; any serious play about him arouses passions from one side or the other. In drama, facts must be coloured by dramatic licence. Any playwright worth his salt has his personal bias – and this will break through into his writing. Actors, too, when they portray a figure famous in history, may have strong opinions about the char-acter they are playing; and this may colour their interpretations, even unconsciously. All of which is contrary to the stern rules of pure documentary, but drama must be allowed its own sort of truth.

Even the greatest lives, the most engrossing moments of history, have their longueurs. The most exciting murder trial is punctuated with pauses and reiterations. Human dialogue is rambling and disorganised, halting with irrelevancies and rarely rising to theatrical moments of climax. Life lacks good lines. Drama cuts away its dull bits, condenses its actions, tidies it up and gives it shape.

Plays in General

Not since the golden age of Hollywood has an entertainment medium been so widely written about as television. Every paper has its TV page, its critics, its television gossip writers. The material is inexhaustible; an endless series of programmes and people. Television grows its pundits overnight – chatshow stars, quizmasters, current affairs moguls, political sports commentators; even the news readers and weathermen acquire their own brand of glamour. Television drama creates its own stars; decades of popular series and soap operas have made unknown actors and actresses into household names with a rapidity impossible in the theatre.

It is an industry with glamour. The studios, to the public, have the same glamour as the backstage; its stars always seem to be just off to film in Italy, or just returning from Los Angeles. Any fact, frivolity or folly about them is news, just as the Hollywood stars could not turn over in bed (so often not their own) without it becoming a matter for wonder.

Happily, television has its serious critics, men and women who have to be poly-talented, expected to report intelligently on everything from *Love's Labour's Lost* to a Conservative Party Conference. They are good and responsible drama critics, whose support of serious TV drama has been constant and important; their voices often at their strongest in defence of the single play.

It is curious how an overall public image can get out of kilter. I can remember times when the viewer, and some writers, seemed bent on dismissing all television plays as belonging to the stark kitchen sink genre, obsessed with human vice, joyless, set in dark cellars, or dirty backrooms, squalid slums or strip clubs. The more romantic side of life seemed confined to the television series. It was for this reason, amongst others, that I changed the title of *The Wednesday Play* to *Play for Today*, to give drama's most important strand a fresh public image, and bring back the viewers that had seemingly strayed away from it.

Socially inspired plays, stark or otherwise, have always been but a part of any annual output, and a relatively small one at that. If they are jewels in the dramatic crown, there are other gems to dazzle us. There have been romantic modern plays in abundance, just as there have been the classic equivalents of *Play for Today* – Webster's *Duchess of Malfi*, for instance, Ford's *'Tis Pity She's a Whore* or Middleton's *The Changeling* – plays as bleak and painfilled as any modern social drama.

Many viewers (particularly the middle-aged) look for well-defined stories, ending happily or tragically, but at least *ending*. The television years have been full of them: Peter Nichol's *The Gorge* and *The Common*. Dennis Potter's *Traitor* and *Where Adam Stood*, John Bowen's *Robin Redbreast*, Roy Minton's *Horace*, Tom Clarke's *Stocker's Copper* and *Mad Jack*, William Trevor's *The General's Day*. Mike Leigh's *Nuts in May*, Peter Terson's *The Fishing Party* and *Stratford or Bust*, Trevor Griffiths' *Through the Night* and *All Good Men*, Jack Rosenthal's *The Evacuees* and *Bar Mitzvah Boy*, Julian Mitchell's *Abide With Me*, Tom Stoppard's *Professional Foul*, Brian Clark's *The Saturday Party* and *The Country Party*. All original, though some of them derived from novels or biographies.

Theatre Plays

Television plays drama demand a continuing flow of new ideas and fresh approaches. A diet of old success and safe formula leads to enervation and death by dramatic starvation. Theatre history is landmarked with such periods of managerial complaisance and a fear of bold innovation.

Television academics may insist that the true purpose of television is immediacy; and that is certainly true for news and current affairs. But the British public have not been going to the play for centuries to learn the facts of life. Usually, they have gone to forget them.

No television drama schedule is complete without some theatre plays, if only because so many of them are excellently written. Even today, when most large towns have their theatres, only a moderate percentage of their population are regular playgoers. Going to the theatre is a matter of choice, an event, and there must still be hundreds of thousands who have never seen *Othello* or *Arms and the Man* or *The Rivals* in a playhouse.

Television has the unique opportunity of giving this huge audience its first glimpse of the great plays, and, to its credit, there has been an unbroken flow of them over the years. At this moment the BBC is two-thirds of the way through its mammoth commitment to produce all the thirty-seven plays of Shakespeare, a happy task spread over six years.

Many theatrical plays transfer naturally to the small screen. They can be edited, cut down a little (for television audiences are impatient) and actually gain by being scenically spread. The very advantage of the medium, its intimacy and closeness, its ability to underline the great performances with its cameras, can discover new qualities in the old masterpieces.

The classic plays have not survived over the centuries by accident, and there should always be a place for one more production, to delight the newest generation. I doubt if many would agree with what William Prynne, a joyless Puritan pamphleteer, wrote in 1633:

'Pity it is to see how many ingenious youths and girls, how many gentlemen and gentlewomen of birth and quality, as if they were born for no other purpose but to consume their youth, their lives in lascivious dalliances, plays and pastimes, sinfully riot away the very cream and flower of their years, their days in playhouses ... all ages, all places have constantly suspected the chastity, yea, branded the honesty of those females who have been so immodest as to resort to theatres, to stage plays, which either find or make them harlots; inhibiting married wives and virgins to resort to plays ...'

A bleak philosophy, and very bad writing.

The play is the root of all drama. However well written the series or the serial adaptation of great novels (many of which are done by the writers of plays), it is the single play, in any medium, that is the cradle of it all. Here will be first tentative efforts of the young playwright, for his local theatre, for the fringe, for television.

If this market shrinks, by the loss of even a few plays, by that much will the overall quality of television drama be diminished.

4

The Writer: The Series

The weekly series is a broadcasting invention, first heard in radio, and developed by television. It is a unique form. Plays have existed as long as civilisation. There were serial films in the cinema – short adventures shown on Saturday mornings, packed with impossible action, each episode ending always with the heroine in peril, tied to a railway line or hanging from a steep cliff, from which the term 'cliffhanger' derives. There was a delightful innocence about these early film series; no sex, no subtlety. Women were either sweetly virginal or middle-aged, men were clean limbed or villainous. The hero was always in danger, loaded with chains in a flooding cellar, with a bomb fizzing nearby to make sure of the job. The directors were not concerned with reality. They knew that a week was a long time in the artistically uncritical lives of their audience, and the survival of the hero was explained each week with the convenient phrase: 'With one bound, our hero was free . . .' Absurd though they were, these films were the forerunners of the weekly television series.

Everything in television has developed rapidly, from its screen time to its sophistication; not least in its habits and conventions. Audience loyalty has ever been one of its prime preoccupations – the gaining, and holding, of the viewer's attention. The great cinema chains vied with each other by offering bigger and better attractions – the normal weekly fare was two films, a cartoon, a newsreel, plus several variety acts and a tedious recital from a monster cinema organ.

Radio established its audience loyalty on a weekly pattern, transmitting popular programme strands at the same hour on the same day, every week. The importance of not varying the hour and day is beyond question; nothing infuriates a loyal viewer or listener more than switching on and finding that his favourite programme has gone out an hour earlier than usual.

Television followed the radio pattern. Series drama was a product of American network television, whose moguls banned the 'continuing story' or serial (except the more fatuous soap operas which could be picked up or put down at random without loss of attention) with the great wet-blanket condemnation: 'You miss one episode, you're lost. Who knows what happened a week ago?' A week in television is admittedly a long time, but one wonders at the acute shortness of the American viewer's memory.

The series format was the answer. It was simple and remorseless. Each week the same characters – policemen, doctors, barristers, cowboys – completed an adventure. Every seven days they tackled one of life's insuperable problems, and it had been solved by the forty-seventh minute. Each series episode was virtually a complete play, leaving no loose ends to be tidied up in the next.

It was a format that allowed little development. The very sameness of the characters, their behaviour and mannerisms, their minor faults and major virtues, was a main part of the attraction. Viewers would have been disorientated by any important changes. They would have been deeply upset if their much admired Chief Detective-Inspector suddenly developed an uncontrollable lust for his sergeant's wife; which, in real life, might happen to anyone.

Originally the format of the series was to serve up the mixture as before, the only real developments being marriage, promotion, and the occasional death of a character who has outlived his usefulness to the format or who has become, as an actor, impossible to work with any longer. Once, in the long-running twice weekly – *The Newcomers* – we arranged for the elimination of a whole batch of characters in a multiple road accident.

BBC television series were established by the sixties, with titles like *Maigret, Doctor Finlay's Casebook* and *Z Cars*; all were written to a strict formula. They were excellent entertainment, well acted and directed, and scripted by some of the finest television writers of the decade – Troy Kennedy Martin, John McGrath, John Hopkins, Keith Dewhurst, Alan Plater, Allan Prior, Robert Barr, Giles Cooper, John Elliot and others.

At their best, they were comparable with any television drama of the time; the standard was high and they pleased millions. But at their worst, drama series were, and are, drama's least spectacular child. The bad ones are facile, repetitious, non-developing, cliché-ridden and predictable: they are improbable in content and resolution, with their leading characters frozen into performances from which they deviate at their peril. The writers of such series must accept a format they can hardly admire, and characterisations as thin as the paper on which the scripts are reluctantly written.

There have been scores of excellent series. But it is a form only too easily debased. Many series are allowed to run on too long, usually in packages of thirteen episodes to fit the quarters of the year, one of television's more meaningless conventions. They are retained because they are still getting good audiences, even though they have become repetitive and run-down, and the better writers have begun to shun them.

There is a moment of truth when even the best series must finish, and deciding that moment is the responsibility of the drama administrator, for television managements will always be loath to bid farewell to anything whilst it has a breath of life left in it. In spite of this, many series outlive their early quality and reputation.

Actors fall into the same trap. They outstay their time, understandably tempted by the regular weekly salaries. They begin to 'freewheel' their performances, trotting out the same attitudes and reactions each week, secure in the knowledge that they will be accepted. They frequently begin to parody their original performances, exaggerating the characteristics that first made them popular.

The actor, or actress, who stays too long is in professional danger. An actor who plays Dr Whatsit in that unstoppable hospital series *It's Me Legs, Doctor* for years, will inevitably *become* Dr Whatsit in the public eye, and no director will want to cast him as anything else. There are two excellent rules for the actor who has stayed too long in a series – grow a beard, or get into a long run in the theatre.

Even at its best, the television weekly series has its absurdities. The police inspector who solves a major crime each week, the barrister who never loses a case, the doctor with the universal cure for everything, including death; these are all merely a parody of life. Skilful writing, acting and direction may cover these weaknesses, but they become startling evident when the work is less than competent.

Many series have been built on dishonest foundations. Their hopeful creators fix on a profession, for example, lifeboats, or tax inspectors, or pawn-brokers. They then manufacture cardboard characters and situations to fit the profession. It is a sure recipe for the third rate, for good drama starts with people, with the weaknesses and strengths of their characters.

The creators of that notable series *Z Cars* (to give an early example) started with a powerful set of characters – the four policemen in the cars, plus a detective inspector and sergeant to control them. All six were highly individual – they had backgrounds, domestic troubles, girl friends, debts and weaknesses. All six became public figures. The names of Fancy Smith, Jock, Steele, Lynch, Barlow and Watt were nationally famous; as well known and admired as that of Jack Warner's George Dixon in *Dixon of Dock Green*.

But all too often I have been sent the other sort of series, sloppy and ill thought-out. They arrive in expensively-bound folders, loaded with irrelevant graphic designs and photographs, and printed on very thick paper. The accompanying letter is always brisk and man-to-man: 'I enclose the layout for our new series – *Stubbs*. Midland Television were all set to produce it, but their budgets were suddenly cut. When you read it, I am convinced you will understand why they were so keen to proceed with it.'

Page One of the brochure is brief: 'Stubbs is a man haunted by his past, the failure of his marriage, his estrangement from his children. He joins the Fire Service to re-establish himself in his own, and in the world's, eyes.'

Page Two is a further description of Stubbs: 'Stubbs could be almost any age, he is young/old. Life has left him deeply embittered, but he laughs often. He is cruel and unrelenting, but is capable of great kindness. He has courage, but knows fear. He gives an impression of tallness, but could be short and stocky. The ideal casting is either Peter Ustinov or Michael Caine.' Or any other actor foolish enough to take it on.

In the past decade, series television has moved further and further from its original rigid formula. Writers began to chafe at a form which allowed so little development, which demanded that no situation should last longer than fifty minutes.

If good characters make good scripts, they argued, then those characters must be allowed to develop naturally and dramatically; and to achieve this, situations must be allowed to continue through a number of episodes. It was not enough for, say, an eminent QC to fail inexplicably in a cut-and-dried murder case; the reasons leading up to the failure must be shown, and the events resulting from it. If a policeman is shown to be dishonest and taking bribes, this weakness should have been hinted at in earlier episodes, not sprung suddenly and improbably on the viewer. One of the strengths of the long running series should be its opportunity to examine human failure and success in detail.

During the seventies, the steady pressure from writers, producers and directors changed the face of the series. With a typically British compromise, it became the series-al: a long running series with a strongly built-in continuing element, which at the same time skilfully gave the impression of offering a complete story each week. Series-al like *The Onedin Line, When The Boat Comes In, Secret Army* and *Angels* are good examples.

There are strong 'series-proper' still to be seen; the Americans in particular persist in the old format. But the compromise has been rewarding. The series-al, by emulating its sister-in-art, the true serial, has taken the good points of both, and has found with them a new and richer quality.

5
The Writer: The Serial

The simple definition of a serial is that it is a prolonged drama, punctuated by regular moments of truth at the end of each episode. Television serials are popular. Viewers have always liked a format that tempts them to return next week for more. *The Forsyte Saga* swept away what had been a brief period of unpopularity for serials by becoming an unbreakable weekly date with viewers all over the world. In Holland clergymen complained it was emptying their churches.

The serial has many faces – thrillers, children's adventures, science fictions and soap opera, and, a broadcasting tradition that began in radio, and was inevitably adopted by television, adaptations of the great classic novels.

The Classic Adaptation

They abounded in the early days of television – Jane Austen, Trollope, the Brontës, the Russian writers – each novel usually mysteriously compressed into six half-hour episodes, however fat or thin the original work. Dickens was a natural choice as so many of his novels were written in weekly parts and thus provided ideal dramatic cutting points.

The lack of new writing encouraged this abundance. Yet such is the popularity of the classics that, even now when original drama is a normal ingredient of the viewers' diet, the demand for dramatisations is as strong as ever.

Colour television gave a spur to the costume serial; dresses that had formerly been mere shades of grey burst into elegant hues, backgrounds took on a new brilliance. Everyone went round assuring each other wisely that 'colour was natural, monochrome was not'. We soon noticed that pastel shades worked better than garish colours, that a bowl of bright red roses in the bottom left-hand corner of the screen drew the eye from actor and performance; (the actors noticed even sooner). We were almost childishly delighted to see our work in colour, nowhere more so than with the three first costume serials in 1968 – *Vanity Fair*, *Portrait Of A Lady*, and John Hopkins' adaptation of Dostoievski's *The Gambler*, with a rare television appearance by Dame Edith Evans.

At that time I was Head of the Serials Drama Department, and the producer of the classic strand, David Conroy, was as determined as I to bring a new look to the classic serial. There still hung over it a blanket of Victoriana, admittedly the richest of literary centuries, and the adaptations were sometimes less exciting than the originals. Too often Jane Austen emerged as 'pretty', the Brontës as 'romantic'. David and I began to schedule as many modern classics as possible, and the next couple of years included Aldous Huxley's *Point Counter Point* and *Eyeless in Gaza*, Compton Mackenzie's *Sinister Street*, Arnold Bennett's *Imperial Palace*, R. H. Mottram's *The Spanish Farm*, Stella Gibbons' enchanting *Cold Comfort Farm* (the title sequences of which could have got us all arrested for obscenity had they been one iota more suggestive), Kazantakis' *Christ Recrucified* and, truly exciting, a thirteen-part adaptation of Jean-Paul Sartre's three novels, *The Age of Reason*, *The Reprieve*, and *Iron in the Soul*, produced under the general title of *The Roads to Freedom*, vividly adapted by David Turner, and boldly directed by James Cellan Jones. In more ways than one, this was a landmark, for it demonstrated convincingly the necessity of including major modern novels in the classic strand. Only the difficulty of obtaining television rights diverted us from Graham Greene and Evelyn Waugh, both of whom were dear to our hearts.

For the programme scheduler, adaptation brings the bonus of well-known titles that carry their message to the viewer before transmission. But their excellence can be a trap to the writer who thinks he need do no more than transpose the 'conversations' of the novel *en bloc* into dramatic speeches; inevitably he will end up disappointingly short of the original. The exquisite rolling phrases of George Eliot may turn out to be, at best, non-dramatic and, at worst, unspeakable by the unfortunate actor.

The late Jack Pulman, when he came to dramatise the two Robert Graves novels into the twelve-episode *I, Claudius* found that the books contained remarkably little usable dialogue. He had to invent twelve hours of Roman conversation, speeches suited equally to slave and Emperor, at the same time preserving the original flavour of the novels; that he succeeded so well is one more tribute to his skill.

Adaptation demands resolution from the writer. He must have a respect for the work he is dramatising, but he must avoid over-reverence. Such blind faith results in the original fire being doused by a heavy shower of ponderously literary transpositions.

The experienced adaptor must first soak himself in the novel, reading it, and re-reading it, bolstering this with other work from the same author. He must consider how he would have approached the task had he been asked to make a television version of his own novel. How would Emily Brontë have translated *Wuthering Heights* to the screen? He must be bold, ready to cut vigorously if it seems necessary, to transpose one part of the story to another, to hold back or advance moments of truth, even to add. He may choose to eliminate characters altogether. Classic novels are often crowded canvases; minor characters slip in and out of the narrative, disappearing altogether for a hundred pages. The novelist can easily reintroduce them with a paragraph, but the viewer will have lost all memory of them for weeks.

Television cannot always match the huge sweep of the great classics. *War and Peace* sends armies marching across its pages; television must be content with regiments, even companies. The TV screen is small, and its domestic picture often far from perfect. Television drama is a foreground matter, with actors communicating close to a very personal audience. But there is a point where sparse economy must be discouraged. The television viewer has been visually spoiled by the extravagancies of old feature films, with their vast crowds and gigantic settings. The streets of a television Dickensian London must not look as empty as if there had been some terrible disaster, and it is no longer enough to represent the Battle of Waterloo by three dead soldiers, one riderless horse, and a Crimean War cannon. An artistic course must be laid between prudence and parsimony.

Most good adaptations will depart, one way or another, from the original, each medium – film, stage or television – adding its own characteristics to the dramatisation. The famous film of *Wuthering Heights*, starring Laurence Olivier, was far from the truth of Emily Brontë's novel. A recent BBC television serial was so close to it that it became almost impenetrable, and lost popular support by its very authenticity; the ideal being, presumably, between the romanticism of the film and the gaunt realism of the television serial.

The television adaptation may offer the viewer his first experience of a great novel, and for this reason alone, dramatisation must be as true as is compatible to a television presentation to the intentions of the original. If alterations are necessary, they must be boldly made. What matters is that the original quality comes through.

The Modern Novel

For television purposes the contemporary novel falls into two classes – those novels actually dealing with the modern scene and those with historical backgrounds; from Graves' *I, Claudius*, through H. E. Bates' *Fair Stood the Wind for France*, or Daphne Du Maurier's *Rebecca* to R. F. Delderfield or John Le Carré. The dramatisation of the period novels should follow precisely the same principles as for the acknowledged classics – a concern for the original tempered by fluidity of adaptation.

Novels of the present may be given an authentic background not always possible for period serials. *Tinker, Tailor, Soldier, Spy*, the BBC adaptation of the Le Carré novel, is a good example of what can be done. In the novel George Smiley walks across Primrose Hill with one of his colleagues; in the television version, he took precisely the same path. But even in this ancient and well-preserved country, historical filming is rarely as authentic. The most perfect Elizabethan manor has its festoon of television aerials. Stonehenge is ringed by modern railings, and the rolling Victorian countryside is marred by power pylons. Sound and the recording of dialogue is equally perilous. Location filming attracts instant and vociferous crowds, even on the most remote Northumberland moor: and aircraft are no respecters of Jacobean verse.

The Hollywood moguls solved the matter by acquiring hundreds of acres of 'lot' around their studios, and simply building what they required – the Tower of London, Renaissance Florence ('Gee, Michelangelo, will you stop chipping away at that old statoo and come to bed?') or the Battle of Gettysburg. This, combined with a benign climate and a generous cash flow, made almost anything possible. Our own climate and budgets make this opulence difficult, but television drama is still noted for the authenticity of its period backgrounds. There are Georgian houses in plenty, Dickensian river wharves, and the Royal Naval College at Greenwich served admirably as the St Petersburg of *Crime and Punishment*.

Very much in fashion, over the last decade, have been serials based on the royal, the famous and the notorious, sometimes all three together. The BBC had its *Henry VIII*, with his wives conveniently providing the standard six-part series; this was quickly followed by *Elizabeth R.*, *Casanova* and *The First Churchills*; by *Edward the Seventh*, *Prince Regent*, *Edward and Mrs Simpson*, *Lillie Langtry*, *Nancy Astor* – all projects based not so much on any particular biography, as on a mass of common public knowledge.

With such projects, the writer has a freer hand. He is not bound to the pages of a classic novel; it is undoubtedly true that the further back he goes into history the bolder can be his invention. What Queen Elizabeth said to the Earl of Leicester on the night of the Armada is not recorded, but a responsible invention will offend no one. Nevertheless, there must be some respect for the subject; to invent a seventh wife for *Henry VIII*, or a husband for Elizabeth is hardly acceptable, though dramatically tempting. Real persons in history, be they Crippen, Charlemagne or Caligula, must be allowed their own credibility. The writer who does less diminishes his work, and his subject.

The family saga has always had a generous place in television. They tend to be of a pattern, spanning several reigns, often beginning in the lamplit, fog-bound, late Victorian world, and progressing through several generations, the Boer War and the First World War providing dramatic punctuations and logical bereavements. The families get either richer or poorer, usually the former. The sons are ever in revolt against their stubborn, conservative fathers, and in the background there is always a tempestuous gypsy-like girl (red headed) who puts the sexual cat amongst the family's prudish pigeons.

These sagas, the most famous of which remains *The Forsyte Saga*, have aristocratic, middle-class, industrial or bucolic backgrounds. The serials have an extraordinary fascination for the viewers, who identify eagerly with the struggles between father and son, mother and daughter. The success of such serials as Winston Graham's *Poldark*, R. F. Delderfield's *A Horseman Riding By*, and *To Serve Them All Our Days*, or Susan Howatch's *Penmarric* is entirely understandable.

*   *   *

Thrillers

Thrillers are the oldest form of serials, and perhaps the most natural choice for them, with their cliff-hangers and counterplots. The 1950s were peppered with six-part thrillers by Francis Durbridge (his first two were *The Broken Horseshoe* and *Operation Diplomat* in 1952), of Giles Cooper, Berkley Mather, Michael Gilbert and Donald Wilson. They derived (via radio) from a long tradition of theatre thrillers and mystery novels that reached a peak of popularity between the wars. The detective mystery is comparatively recent in literature – the mid-nineteenth century saw its birth with Edgar Allan Poe, and later with Wilkie Collins (*The Moonstone* and *The Woman in White*), with Sheridan LeFanu and Charles Dickens; later still with Conan Doyle's *Sherlock Holmes*, which set a pattern that is still followed.

Radio was quick to see the advantages of the thrillers as audience grabbers; from the early thirties they were a regular part of broadcasting. After the war, Francis Durbridge's *Paul Temple* and the daily *Dick Barton* were at the top of the listening polls.

Thriller serials, as opposed to the hard-edged crime series, are ideal entertainment for the tired viewer who doesn't want to be taxed too hard after a bad day at the office. They are exciting without being frenetic. The characters are recognisable, the women either wholesomely or wickedly beautiful, the heros lean and durable, the crooks well groomed, slightly out of condition, and heading for alcoholism if the size of their drinks is anything to go by. The villains tend to be unfairly rich, possessed of huge cars, and give a distinct impression, until the final denouement, that crime *does* pay. The police are polite in a deadly sort of way, a mask that slips at the end of the last episode. These serials only lightly challenge their audience – they produce subtle clues to help you spot the villain, but it doesn't matter if you don't. The more sadistic areas of crime are not dwelt upon; from time to time people are shot, in an aseptic sort of a way, a neat round hole in a vital part, but no mess on the carpet.

Naturally the thriller has gained in sophistication over the years. The early Durbridge serials had to make do with a limited filmed content. Today's thriller may be shot entirely on film, anywhere from Barnstaple to Barcelona. But the old flavour lingers. The first episode poses the mystery, introduces the cast and murders one of them. The second raised doubts about what you thought to be a nice straightforward murder, and hints at personal complications amongst the cast. The next episodes kill off several more actors, mounting through a tension of false confession and counter-accusation. The last episode leads to a boisterous climax, with everyone chasing each other in cars, boats or helicopters; a few more people are shot, leaving the residue of the cast to explain what all the fuss was about. An entirely satisfying form of entertainment.

Crime and police series, over the past decade, have taken a harder route, with the anti-hero as king. Or shabby private investigators sailing just to windward of the law; detectives with dubious pasts and doubtful futures. Vicious crooks, using all the aids of technology, manoeuvring with millions in the international scene. As in crime feature films, the action has steadily become harsher, the violence more casual, the pain thrust harder at the audience. The danger of this formula is that it must be ever building on its own characteristics. What is shocking in one episode (or one film) must be doubly shocking in the next, the pain must be that much more explicit. In the cinema, this has meant an endless cycle of extremely violent films.

Violence may be allowed to go unchecked in feature films, but it cannot be accepted for television. The public elect to go to the cinema, pay on the spot for the privilege; if they chose a particularly violent film, that is their choice. But television is piped into people's homes and, though there are safeguards against excess (see Chapter 11) there can be no sure way of knowing who is in front of a television set at any hour, however late.

The only true safeguard is a responsible, sometimes unwritten, code of practice between programme makers, writers, directors and administrators; a code which demonstrates concern for audience and content, and the handling of that content.

It is not without significance that while the Francis Durbridge type of thriller serials are consistently well up in the viewing ratings, many crime and police series that stepped over the borders of violence disappeared unmourned. There have been excellent 'anthology' series, each week completing one mystery: *Detective* presented a weekly dramatisation of a detection novel. *Sherlock Holmes*, that most revived of all private investigators, did the same. But most popular are those genuine thriller serials, close-packed with cliff-hangers and red herrings. The worst of them may be regrettable; the best bring pleasure to all but the sourest of drama snobs.

*   *   *

Children's Serials

Television has always provided drama for children; one of the oldest BBC strands is the Family Classic, firmly rooted at tea time on Sundays, when the whole family from nine to ninety might be gathered for relaxation; a durable strand, stretching back thirty years, often in the form of a dramatised children's classic, sometimes Dickens or Scott or Stevenson, sometimes original serials written for this genre.

The children's serial has its own rules, proprieties and mythology – some written, some understood through long custom. Its conflicts must be boisterous rather than violent, sex is holding hands, bad language is out. The strand has always been a sort of moral touchstone for those who guard the young viewer (sometimes unneccessarily) against the harms of television. Yet no strand has been more consistently and carefully produced for a particular audience. Young entertainment calls for action and adventure, whether it is the jolly knockabout of Robin Hood and that all-time loser, the Sheriff of Nottingham, or the darker violence of Charles Dickens, which is often more mental than physical. Victorian writers did not shrink from chilling young blood – *Tom Brown's Schooldays* is full of pain and misery, and every school story had its unpopular pupil who had to endure the agonies of bullying and ostracism. Dickens bitterly reflected his own childhood poverty and near-starvation; yet his novels have always been prime favourites for the Family Classic serials, providing as they do a rich mixture of adventure, sentiment and humour.

In children's drama the important factor is the way in which the work is done, and that, in television, lies very much in the hands of the director. A violent scene can be shot in a dozen ways, only one of which will cause fear or offence. The trick, with the young audience, is to convey the suffering and strife without causing nightmares.

Children's drama requires a simplicity of story-line and presentation, avoiding the oblique. Complicated personal relationships, Freudian obsessions, and the darker sides of human nature are better left out. They will be lost anyway on the young viewer, with his enviable capacity for ignoring what he does not understand. Add to this formula short scenes, a measure of action and motion, a small and recognisable cast, and there you have the bones of the children's serial.

There are traps for the uninitiated. The writer who writes *down* to his young audience, the actor who acts down, is doomed from the start; children recognise condescension, even if they cannot properly define it. Nor does a straightforward approach and a simple presentation mean a reduction of standards to infantile proportions. The writer must understand his particular audience; he can assume an eager desire for enjoyment, as the young viewer has not had time to become blasé. But he must not trade on their lack of sophistication. He must aim slightly above their heads, and give full value; no cheap tricks to impress, no nightmare images. Children will accept any amount of fighting and strife provided the protagonists and the issues are clearly identified.

They, moreover, will more readily accept grim situations in costume drama, having the mental escape route that 'It happened in those days, but couldn't today'. Modern drama is a different matter. When Father quarrels bitterly with Mother, gives her a black eye, and walks off into the night, that is an identifiable situation, and may cause the child viewer to brood on the security of family and home every time his parents have a mild row. Music has a powerful effect. A scene in a haunted manor, with a transparent ghost hovering about may leave the young viewer unmoved. Add creepy music, and his emotions may be raised to a pitch that is at first uncomfortable, and soon frightening. No director of children's drama should underestimate the power of music.

The subject is all-important. Adaptations of the young Victorian and Edwardian classics have been surprisingly popular with succeeding generations – *Little Women*, *A Little Princess*, *Katy*, *Heidi* and the E. Nesbitt books are prime favourites with the girls; for boys, the adventures of Robert Louis Stevenson – *Treasure Island* and *Kidnapped* – are remade regularly and the novels of Walter Scott, whom I find unreadable in prose form, but which transfer with gusto to the screen. Classic heroes like King Arthur, Richard the Lionheart and Robin Hood are permanent favourites. But classics are not enough: there must be modern serials like *Grange Hill*, *William Brown*, *Wurzel Gummidge*.

Dramatisations of children's novels, which include heroes, like Jim Hawkins and Tom Brown, have held young viewers for decades. They bring more than entertainment, they offer a glimpse of good writing, and may guide their audience to the original novels; not as set books to be laboured through at school, but as sources of genuine pleasure and delight.

Science Fiction

I have to confess that most science fiction bores me. I can appreciate the John Wyndham type novels, with their sense of history and destiny, or the Ray Bradburys and Arthur Clarkes, which are well written. I have also an abiding soft spot for the BBC's unique *Doctor Who*, a science fiction for the family that has mixed humour with galactic fireworks for eighteen years. But in general I find the genre monotonous, unrewarding, and frequently ludicrous. The plots are flimsy hat-racks for electronic effects, model-work and television trickery. The stories have an uninspiring sameness: some nasty person/mutant/monster is determined to take over the country/world/universe, and to achieve this destroys everyone in sight with unfair weapons.

The backgrounds are bleak and utilitarian – moonscapes and dark caverns, intercut with the interior of spaceships ablaze with winking lights to which no one, least of all the gallant commandant, pays the smallest regard. The inhabitants of this joyless world are usually dressed in silver tracksuits and, like cowboys, never eat or sleep, being sustained by the occasional drink (bright purple) and virtue. I admit that I envy them the simplicity of their lives – no Income Tax, rates, bills, school fees – just an occasional tussle with a monster or a collision between planets.

Most science fictions have monsters, ranging from the sophisticated Daleks to awakened mummies, giant insects and amorphous masses. These monsters have one thing in common – a perfect knowledge of English, which, though metallically monotonous, helps to keep the plot moving.

But this (as you will have concluded) is personal bias. Science fiction is successful. It brings excitement to millions, and certainly taxes the ingenuity of the programme makers. Television sci-fi has to stand comparison with expensive feature films like *Star Wars*, extravaganzas costing millions and having the advantage of every film trick in the book. There is no mystique about such super-epics – you just need a lot of money, a lot of nerve, and the best technicians in the business. Television's brief is simpler, and more difficult, because nothing looks shoddier than a cut-price science fiction. You can do *Hamlet* in black drapes and rostrums, and no one will complain; you will probably be hailed as having achieved a dramatic breakthrough. But science fiction won't work without exotic backgrounds, special properties and high-quality models. It is a fantasy land that has to convince. *Star Wars* can concentrate all its resources and energies into one vast effort. Television must repeat the trick week after week, and build on itself as it goes. Considering the limitations, the results are astonishingly good. The followers of science fiction are addicts to a man, and no television impresario can afford to ignore so passionately dedicated an audience.

Soap Opera

The name derives from the giant American soap and detergent firm – Proctor and Gamble – whose ample money has backed many a marathon weekly/twice weekly/thrice weekly series in the States. The term has become somewhat slighting, inferring less than the best, and the recent American series *Soap* is an ironic derivation.

Television drama has its levels, and bad soap opera may be said to plumb the dramatic depths. But there are good soaps, too. They have their own rules of construction. The story-lines must be broad-based, allowing for endless development. A large firm, a big store, a boarding house are good backgrounds, permitting a varied cast of characters to meet and mingle, work and love together. A desert island, on the other hand, peopled by the five survivors from a wreck, would present problems. Soap thrives on a wide canvas, and there is a special skill in keeping all the strands moving along together, allowing the public at least a glimpse of the major characters each week, lest they be forgotten. If a glimpse is impossible, they must at least be referred to, and a lot of soap dialogue concerns the activities of people off-screen.

Soap is a general term which is often wrongly applied. I have heard, for example, R. F. Delderfield's *A Horseman Riding By*, James Mitchell's *When the Boat Comes In* and *All Creatures Great and Small* all referred to as 'good soap'. None of these serials had the soap characteristics.

True soap – whether it be weekly, twice or thrice weekly – may be profuse in plot, but it must be simple in presentation, capable of casual viewing by the family while it is completing its meal. The stories must progress slowly, ensuring that anyone who misses a couple of episodes can pick up the threads without difficulty. One often gets the impression, coming back to a soap after a couple of weeks, that nothing has happened at all. The portrayals tend to be basic, relying more on the personality of the actors than any deep character examination: yet talented actors can give the worst of parts substance. When in repertory I once managed to say the impossible line 'You blind, blind fool, Philip Cunningham, to think that she would ever wed the like of you' without the audience laughing.

Television has never lacked for soap opera. The earliest BBC TV soap was *The Grove Family*, whimsically named after the television studios at Lime Grove. This was the most basic of soaps, the family unit. Granny Grove, a lovable old curmudgeon, Father Grove, long-suffering about electricity bills, Mother, sons, daughters, friends – debts and taxes, sweethearts and marriages, births and death, emerging twice a week (live) from Lime Grove's tiniest studio.

Later there was *Compact* (woman's magazine, affectionately known as *Compost*), *The Flying Swan* (hotel/guest house) and one of the more enduring, *The Newcomers*. This was an ideal formula, based on the national movement of light industry from the cities into semi-country towns like Thetford in Norfolk. It provided all the ingredients – family uprooted into new environment, the problems of adjustment, the resistance of the residents to change, town against country, problems with farming, crop failure, teenagers, the local newspaper – enough to over-feed a serial for years; which it did. Running alongside *The Newcomers* was its stablemate – *United* – so that, between the two, they provided 200 thirty-minute episodes a year, rehearsing and recording sixty minutes each week. It sounds back-breaking and spirit-crushing; in fact *The Newcomers* ran like clockwork. It had a very talented cast, large enough to allow time off and ensure that no one character had too much weight to carry (or too many lines to learn). It grew into a most contented community who allowed for each others' irritating habits and hardly quarrelled at all.

Independent Television, however, must take the gold for the most successful long-running soap of all time – *Coronation Street*, Granada's irreplaceable twice weekly. After twenty years, it has retained its sparkle, its energy and its tart Lancastrian flavour; it has a corporate air of confident enjoyment that is unique.

As far as the writing goes, soaps are sound professional work. A separate story-line writer works well ahead with the producer, setting up developments of plot and characters, periodically starting new hares: will they build the ring road? Must the old Manor House come down? Is Charlie going to marry Vivienne at last? Every situation is milked dry, spread through as many episodes as can credibly be accepted. *The Newcomers* had, and *Coronation Street* has, the same over-riding strength – that of the close-knit community.

As a subject *United* was less happy. At first sight, it might have appeared a sure winner; a professional football team in a largish town, the lives of the players, problems with their own and other peoples' wives, promotion, relegation, transfers, thick-headed managers and swollen-headed players, fan clubs and boardrooms – all the human stuff of the national game. Unfortunately, it lacked one vital ingredient. Professional footballers are at their most exciting playing first-class football to crowded stands. Most actors have difficulty in kicking a ball credibly, let alone at high professional standard; and the resources of a twice weekly soap do not extend to filling stadiums with cheering extras. Consequently, *United* was short on football, and strong on personal problems, few of which seemed related to the game.

Lack of filmed content, exterior action scenes, is the common disease of the soap opera; the rate of strike, two episodes a week, leaves little time outside rehearsal room or studio. *Coronation Street*, of course, has its whole street permanently built at Granada.

The Brothers was a glossy BBC long-runner, based on the activities of a road transport company; it ran to seven series over four years. The opening episodes were rich with lorries grinding in and out of transport cafés and parking lots, lumbering dramatically along motorways. Later episodes had to be content with an impression of thundering transport, whilst the story was acted out in boardroom and home. This in no way inhibited the huge success of the serial. It is people who make drama interesting, not vehicles. *The Brothers* had all the qualities of good soap – successful men and beautiful women, living in newly decorated, immaculate houses. No toys on the floor, no mess, no finger marks under light switches. Affairs in plenty, but neat and aseptic, no sweat. A dream world certainly, but drama has been providing that fantasy for centuries.

There is no artistic law against a soap opera being well acted, written and directed. Unfortunately, there is a financial law that too often denies the means to do the work well. Many soap operas are kept alive long after they have become enervated to the point of expiry, simply because they are still drawing audiences. I myself was criticised for taking off *The Newcomers* while it was still popular. But I knew that it was in decline, that it was better to conclude it when it still had quality, rather than let it slide into mediocrity.

Soap opera is one of television's pillars; it is unintelligent to be dramatically snobbish about a form that the public want. What one must do is make them as good as possible. There are always writers, directors and actors ready to bring this about.

6

The Producer and Script Editor

If television is new, the television producer (as opposed to director) is newer. He (or she, for many of the best are women) is a natural product of the expansion of television. For many years drama directors worked directly to their Departmental Heads, the modesty of the output making this practical. Drama was a compact family, with comfortable family rules. It moved along contentedly in the mock-paternalistic climate enjoyed by British broadcasting since its radio inception in the twenties.

Then came Independent Television, and competition; undoubtedly the best thing that could have happened to the BBC. The arrival of ITV gingered up the former monopoly holders mightily. As most of us in drama had come from the hard competition of the theatre, the appearance of a rival did not disturb us one bit. If anything, it was to our advantage. The value of a director who knew his job was magically inflated overnight.

With competition came expansion, and happily much of it was in drama. So large was the increase that drama had to be carved up into manageable units – television strands. Strands in turn created the need for someone to look after them, and so the television producer was born; a man or woman, responsible for a 'set' of dramas – half a dozen plays, a long-running serial like *The Forsyte Saga*, a series like *Maigret* or *Dr Finlay's Casebook*.

Most producers are responsible for an annual output, the cost of which would make the budgets of the theatrical impresario look like parking fines. In return, a great deal is demanded of him. He is expected to match his writer and director artistically, to understand the financial structure of television, and know how to juggle its resources from one part of his output to another. As a matter of course he must be a good-humoured disciplinarian, capable of soothing an angry star or keeping a wayward director in order; before which, he must have had the personality or reputation to persuade them to come and work for him. It is automatically assumed that he will bring to his strand a style and quality above average, and entirely his own. It is hardly surprising that there is a shortage of such supermen.

The producer in the cinema has existed for years, and some sort of comparison may be drawn between those of the golden Hollywood days, and the producer today in the great television 'houses' – the BBC or the major ITV companies. Hollywood practised paternalism – a ruthless, unsentimental brand – in that the studio maintained large families under one roof; they had their star artists, their writers, their staffs and technicians. They treated their stars well as long as they were successful, and abandoned them at the first hint of failure. They protected them against professional over-exposure and, as far as they knew how, against bad scripts. If one of their actors was found sleeping with a minor, they had formidable legal departments to bury the skeleton. Hollywood studios were entertainment factories of high efficiency – they had their own stages, their acres of 'lot'. They had rows of writers (Moss Hart claimed that the walls of their offices were padded) to listen respectfully to their ideas about scripts; they had their favourite producers.

The Hollywood production route was well marked. The front offices raised the finance for a film from outside sources – the first rule of show business is to lose other people's money – and, once the backing was assured, they handed the project to a producer, with a budget and production schedule. From then on, the producer was responsible, under God and the studio Chief, for the delivery of the film on time and on budget.

Time was money, and if the production fell behind schedule, the front office took steps. Impossible stories are legion. My favourite is the one about the great director John Ford, who was out on location with a Western; he was three days behind schedule, and his producer arrived in a Cadillac and a fret: 'John you're three days behind schedule. What you gonna do about it?' Ford remained calm. He studied his shooting script for a moment, then, at random, tore out twenty pages, 'OK?' he said. 'We're back on schedule.'

Today's Hollywood scene is very different. Producers have long operated as independents, film-making round the world, though they still route their films through the old organisations like Fox, Columbia and Warners, for distribution and so on. The studios still produce films, but their families are long dispersed, and much of their time and effort is given over to television series.

Some of the old Hollywood structure can be found in television; the larger organisations control, under one roof, the planning, writing and production of a huge entertainment output.

But unlike his film counterpart, the television producer is responsible, not for one film, but for a whole set of productions. The film producer had, and still has, the luxury of coping with one project at a time. The television producer must spread his energies, preparing one play, rehearsing a second, overseeing the post-production of a third; a wide productivity that goes far to explain the difference between film and television costs.

At any one time, BBC Television Drama (to take an example) employs about forty-five producers across its production centres in Britain. Between them they father about four hundred dramatic children each year. To understand their jobs properly, one has to fix their position in the management hierarchy.

The public view of the BBC is that of a vast, boring, monolithic bureau, self-perpetuating, over-stuffed with permanent officials, duplicating each other's work in perfect harmony, the only crisis being the non-arrival of the tea trolley.

The truth, as far as the programme-maker is concerned, is more practical. There are only two television 'funnels' into which all their programme ideas can be poured, BBC1 and BBC2, the two national networks – each presided over by a Controller, and supplied by a score of output departments – Drama, Light Entertainment, Sports, Current Affairs, Documentaries, Children's, Music and Arts, Features, Schools, Religion and who knows what.

The Controllers, though God-like, are not monastic, and a running dialogue maintains between them and the heads of these departments across the year, often quite amiably.

BBC Drama is too large to be contained in a single department, and is split into five – two in London (Plays Drama and Series/Serials Drama), one in Birmingham (English Regions Drama) and one each in Scotland and Wales, who, quaintly enough, do Scottish Drama and Welsh Drama. Each Department has a professional Head, an ex-producer/director/writer, and all work to the central governance of a Group. At fixed points in the year departments offer each Channel Controller their ideal mix of production for the financial year ahead; these 'offers' make financial and artistic commitments, which will be agreed and adhered to. There are traditional strands on each channel – the modern plays on BBC1, the classic adaptations on BBC2, the Sunday family serials on BBC1 and so on. The discussions are about content, rather than continuance. This is important, for every department must rely on a certain continuity of output; intelligent drama planning is impossible without it.

Each production has attached to it a document of daunting complexity. This paper spells out the cost of everything in the drama, of the staff and resources required to achieve it. In today's climate of automatic annual inflation, cost estimates for a year ahead are little more than whimsical conjecture – in the BBC they are cynically known as Guesstimates – and the documents are hardly better than a basis for discussion, and for later recrimination when they are proved to be inaccurate. Each department in turn feeds its ingredients into this optimistic annual banquet, and the whole menu is fed into a computer; which mutters to itself and comes up with a predictable 'Impossible'.

Long experience has taught me that all annual programme estimates are impossible, most of all those coming from the greedy, selfish, grasping, impertinent drama departments. What is curious is that most of these 'impossible' programmes get written and produced, costing more than the original estimates, and give general delight. I suspect that managerial outrage at drama costs has always been a formality. Once the programmes succeed and the awards begin rolling in, all is forgiven. This, anyway, is of small importance. What matters is that good work continues to go out to the viewers.

Once accepted, the strand becomes legitimate. The producer is given the go-ahead, the budget, and production and transmission dates that he must meet. The type of strand will decide the route he will take to transmission, the play producer working at a different rhythm to his colleague in series. As drama conveniently falls into artistic divisions, so can we.

The Plays Producer

New plays are important. They are difficult to do consistently well, and it is unlikely that anyone will produce a strand that is immaculate throughout. The television play has a short but battle-scarred history, punctuated by bitter controversy, frequently the object of nervous official suspicion.

The less flexible side of establishment has ever been wary of the new single play, fearful of whom it might offend either politically, socially or morally. There is a convention that all new television playwrights are left-wing, anti-authority, nihilist, fascist, marxist and perverted. Few of them fit these labels. They tend to be young, with the fire of protest in their bellies, and it is not surprising if they are radical and anti-establishment. But I have yet to meet a serious playwright who subscribes to the 'let's destroy it all and build from scratch' philosophy – Arcady from Anarchy.

Good playwrights write drama, not tracts. Plays can be bold, irreverent and unrepentant; they can be light-hearted; they can be socially, morally or politically motivated; they can be classic. What they must not be is cosy in content, or conventional in treatment. A drama department that offends no one is in poor straits. A new play strand is an abrasive operation, and the seat of the television Head of Plays is a hot one.

During my dozen years as Head of the BBC Television Drama Group, I worked with four Heads of Plays, all very different, all indistinguishable in their determination to put their own output first and everyone else's nowhere.

The first was Gerald Savory, a cheerful man whose theatrical experience stretches back to before television was thought of. He has written many successful plays for the theatre, including the record-breaking comedy *George and Margaret*. A television producer for years in America and England, he became a poacher turned gamekeeper in the sixties, and went into drama administration.

There are no *natural* drama administrators, as there are in the business or political world. No young actor or stage manager starts out with the idea of becoming the head of a great theatrical enterprise – the idea would be depressingly middle-aged. All of us have to be persuaded – pressganged might be a better word – into giving up what really delighted us, writing, directing, producing, to take on the dry aggravation of television administration. The amazing thing is we allow ourselves to be caught, for we are quite intelligent.

Gerald, knowing so well his theatre and television, was not to be deceived by poor scripts or sloppy production. As a Departmental Head he had a discerning nose for disaster. I remember him questioning one of his producers, in whom he had only a moderate faith, about how his production had come out. The producer hesitated fatally for a second, then launched into an extravagant paean of praise – the script had come out better than he had hoped, he had never seen such performances, the lighting set a new pattern for the future, the director had surpassed himself. 'When can I see it?' asked Gerald. Another hesitation from the babbling producer, then: 'Well – as soon as the music's been dubbed on. I mean, once the music is on, it'll be – well, you'll see . . .' 'As bad as that?' said Gerald gently.

The producer collapsed and admitted that he had a problem. I loved working daily with Gerald. He is splendidly theatrical, witty, anti-pompous. We share an overdeveloped sense of the ridiculous that has saved both of us from theatrical ulcers.

As a departmental head, he had a courteous disregard for managerial criticism, on the principle that anyone who didn't like drama was hardly worth considering. His taste ranged from Mercer to Molière – he enjoyed and understood both. Superlatively optimistic for 95 per cent of the time, he could be as cast down as the rest of us on occasions.

One of these black moods coincided with a particularly disastrous Offers Meeting (that moment of truth when the channel controller accepts or rejects the drama offerings for the future year). The meeting had ground to a sullen stalemate of non-agreement, and had been adjourned to the following day. Later that evening, Gerald put his head round my door, 'I've made a new Offers document for tomorrow,' he said. 'That's quick,' I said. 'Let's have a look.' Gerald handed me a completely blank piece of paper. 'I shall inform the Controller,' he said with dignity, 'that as he wants nothing from my department, that is what I am now offering him – nothing'! 'Don't do it,' I begged. 'He'll jump at it, and make it the rule from now on.'

Richer thoughts prevailed, and the next day was all sunlight, sweet reason and acceptance. But I've always had a sneaking regret that we didn't try it.

After five years (which include plays from David Mercer, Dennis Potter, Jim Allen, Hugh Leonard, Simon Gray, John Bowen, Jeremy Sandford, John Hopkins, Nigel Kneale, Ian Curteis, Peter Nichols, Tony Parker, Douglas Livingstone, Alun Owen, E. A. Whitehead, Julia Jones, Robert Muller, Roy Minton, Arthur Hopcraft, Rhys Adrian, Willis Hall, Ingmar Bergman, Colin Welland, Clive Exton, John Osborne, and just about everyone else writing at the time) Gerald decided to go back to writing and producing, and has prospered since. His recent scripts of *Dracula* and *Dr Jekyll and Mr Hyde* were notable successes.

He was followed, in 1972, by Christopher Morahan, one of the best television directors of the day, and later Deputy Director of the National Theatre.

To those who don't know him, Chris is a stern figure, who frightens the life out of the irresolute and wayward. He has the highest standards of drama (and conduct) and will not suffer fools or bad work even half-gladly. As a Drama Head he demanded the best, and stoutly supported those who gave it him. I admired him (still do) and soon realised that, once known, he is a warm friend and a staunch colleague. He fathered a vast number of fine plays during his four years in Plays, and I suspect that he enjoyed very much being one of the team of Drama Heads of Department.

When he went off to the National, in 1976, I was joined by James Cellan Jones, another top drama director. Jimmy is Welsh, ebullient, mercurial, courageous, warm hearted and razor sharp, without an ounce of deference for grey establishment figures. We had already worked together in Serials Drama, where he had brilliantly directed *Roads to Freedom* (based on the three wartime novels by Jean-Paul Sartre), Henry James' *Portrait of a Lady*, and *The Golden Bowl*, and a sparkling production of Aldous Huxley's *Eyeless in Gaza*.

In a profession that tempers truth with kindness – 'Marvellous reading, old boy. Never heard Laertes given that particular – er – anyway, don't ring us, we'll ring you,' Jimmy is possessed of a rare honesty; a disconcerting habit of saying precisely what he thinks. I soon learned to appreciate this quality, even when he was telling me how wrong I was.

Jimmy has always been something of an eccentric, particularly in the matter of dress. He spurns ties, preferring a twisted silk scarf. He abhors socks, and even in the coldest weather is seen in open sandals. Soon after his appointment, he was invited to a black-tie dinner with the Governors of the BBC. An anxious member of the Secretariat took me aside: 'He will wear a tie, won't he?' he murmured. 'And socks,' I promised, leaving him even more uneasy. In the event, Jimmy looked more elegant than anyone. His car was equally individual. He drove an ancient, battered open Bristol 'tourer', a vehicle of great solidity unless one sat in the back. The story is that the floorboards had collapsed under the weight of one of drama's stouter producers – Cedric Messina – who suddenly found himself in danger of running rather than riding.

Jimmy's two and a half years was packed with good things. He launched the six-year project to produce all thirty-seven Shakespeare plays; he established *Première*, the thirty-minute film strand that gives young directors their first chance at film-making. He gingered up a somewhat enervated classic *Play of the Month* by including modern 'classics' like David Mercer's *Flint* and Edward Bond's *The Sea*. His time was marked by courageous contemporary work – notably that contentious quartet about police corruption – *Law and Order*. New plays included Trevor Griffiths' moving play about cancer, *Through the Night*, Jack Rosenthal's *Spend, Spend, Spend*, Jim Allen's *The Spongers*, Harold Pinter's *Langrishe Go Down*, and the charming trilogy about J. M. Barrie – *The Lost Boys* – from Andrew Birkin.

Jimmy enjoyed the challenge, and did it faithfully, but he never ceased to yearn after the job he most enjoyed – directing, and in the end, he returned to it. His place was taken by Keith Williams, another Welshman, though this time via Guernsey. Like me, Keith had been through every theatrical hoop – stagehand, stage manager, actor, understudy, director, writer, script editor, producer. To my envy, he had once played Miserable Starky in *Peter Pan*, a Christmas treat enjoyed by my four children in turn. Because I usually knew the actor playing Captain Hook, they each had the bonus of going backstage and trying on the famous hook.

Keith burst over Plays Department like a thunderbolt. He worked all the hours that God sent, and invented a few of his own. Within a few weeks of his arrival, the corridors seemed to be jammed with the best television writers and directors.

It was his misfortune to arrive at a time when BBC finances were at their lowest ebb. The reluctance of successive governments to increase the Licence Fee to cope with an overdraft of tens of millions, and a new Government intent on stern economy, meant that the BBC was forced into illogical cuts: in capital investment – new buildings and equipment – in traditional 'house' orchestras, local radio and, of course, in programmes of every sort, radio and television. This was the time when the oldest broadcasting organisation in the world seemed to be wrong-footed every time, every fault magnified, its virtues overlooked. A poor public image that was to a large extent the fault of the BBC itself, which has always been ludicrously slow at underlining its good points; an almost Freudian distaste for 'boasting' that verges on commercial suicide.

Like Jimmy Cellan Jones, Keith is mercurial, soaring between cloud nine optimism, and black depression. I remember meeting him once when he was at the wrong end of the thermometer: 'I was awake all night,' he confessed. 'Last night's play. Wasn't it awful?'

'Keith,' I said sternly. 'If you let things like that keep you awake, you'll never sleep again.'

The moral of this (if one must have one) is that no unit making scores of plays every year can expect them all to be winners; it is against all theatrical odds.

These four Heads of Plays, over a memorable decade of television, shared one conviction – that it begins with the writers; without good scripts you might as well go out and sell insurance.

A breakdown of the 1979 output of BBC television plays (what an age of statistics we live in) indicated that nearly half the plays of fifty minutes or over were contemporary. In addition, there were six thirty-minute films, all modern, thirteen classic plays including the Shakespeares of that year, four play trilogies, three of which were contemporary, a serialised version of Grossmith's *Diary of a Nobody*, and some dozen assorted dramas, amongst which were two blockbusters – *Churchill and the Generals*, a three-hour play about Winston Churchill and his relationship with the generals of World War Two – and, *Suez*, also three hours, a dramatisation of the political scene leading up to this major historical blunder. Both were written by Ian Curteis, which must surely be a record dramatic double.

An output of about eighty plays, the accent on contemporary drama at the ratio of three to one, balanced against the rest of the Drama Group's output. Such a balance calls for a round-the-year vigilance. I once discovered that the Group was proposing to present, in one week, three dramas about gypsies – a play, a series and a serial episode. I had either to separate them, or declare a National Romany Week.

One of the standard questions at earnest television seminars (which increase by the hour) is 'Where do we find the new producers?' The question itself is usually irrelevant, as it is posed by people who would not know what to do with a new producer if they found one; but the answer is plain enough. Producers can come from all sorts of places, provided they have the talent to understand the job, and the energy and stamina to carry it through successfully. He could be an ex-production assistant who has worked for years in television drama; a script editor who has sat alongside his producer for many seasons, and knows what mistakes to avoid; a television director, or one from the theatre, who has run his own regional company.

Graeme MacDonald became one of television's most successful

producers, after an apprenticeship with Granada, that covered every corner of entertainment. Tony Garnett, Irene Shubik, Andrew Brown and Margaret Matheson were script editors: David Conroy and Graham Benson were production assistants. Richard Eyre ran the Nottingham Playhouse for years, and there gave Trevor Griffiths' *Comedians* its first production; it was later repeated in television. Jonathan Powell, whose credits include *The Mayor of Casterbridge, Tinker, Tailor, Soldier, Spy, Thérèse Raquin* and *Testament of Youth*, was with Granada television as a general producer. So, too, was Mark Shivas, first in their script unit, later as the producer/presenter of *Cinema*. Mark's television credits stretch endlessly from *The Six Wives of Henry VIII*, through *Casanova* and *Telford's Change* to *On Giant's Shoulders* and *The Borgias*. Like most top directors and producers, he has chosen to remain a freelance, moving between BBC, ITV and feature films.

The producer of the acknowledged classic play starts with an advantage – Shakespeare, Shaw or Sheridan has already done much of the work. The producer of the new contemporary play starts from scratch. Stage plays, however well adapted for television, usually bring with them a smell of the theatre and greasepaint; it would actually be foolish to deny their genesis.

It was no accident, as television drama gathered strength, that writers began to concentrate on contemporary plays. There was a swing to reality – as there was in the theatre and novels – of theme and background. Studios became restrictive boxes. The directors wanted to be out and about in the depressing towns of the north, the slums of Glasgow, the suburban deserts. There was a revolt against the middle-class image of drama that had so long been maintained. Out of these rebellions came *Cathy Come Home, In Two Minds, Up The Junction, Vote Vote Vote For Nigel Barton*; plays in incredible contrast to what had gone before them.

The Wednesday Play (under the guise of *Play for Today*) is still alive. In 1979 (a random sample) its two dozen plays came from nearly a dozen producers including those from the regions and Scotland. But more than half came from two London-based producers – Kenith Trodd and Richard Eyre, one a veteran of television, the other in his first year of it.

Whatever his route, let us assume our producer to have arrived. He is sitting in an office as yet bare of reminiscent photographs, with little more than a budget and a secretary. If he has come up through the 'factory floor' of drama, he will already have formed associations with writers and directors. He may have brought with him ideas and scripts of his own creation, or he may be starting with a blank page, though hopefully not a blank mind.

His brief is to supply six plays to the strand and he must decide what his expectations are from them. If there is to be the unity of a linking theme, he must establish what it is – a sextet of, say, plays about racism, broken marriages, teenagers. The danger of uniting themes is that the accidents of television recording and scheduling may eventually split the plays in the transmission plan; so the original intention must be firmly stated, and unyieldingly defended.

It is more likely that the producer will be asked for six plays for the general strand, with no more of a brief than 'to make them contemporary, hard-edged and good.' In which case he is, in a sense, liberated. He can commission on almost any modern topic, provided the producer in the next office has not already had the same idea. Whatever the form, his output must come with his own personal stamp on it, his taste and his convictions. Sitting on the dramatic fence is easy – it is far better to shout aloud one's own views. The viewers may not agree with them but at least they will have heard them.

A plays producer starts work at least six months before his first script is due for rehearsal, by which time, he would be wise to know precisely where he is going with the rest of his commissions; once the recording cycle starts, time gallops withal.

Six months is none too long. The temptation to go for busy established writers is great, partly because you admire them, partly because a new producer is anxious to demonstrate that he is someone with whom the best people work. The experienced writer will not be offended if he or she is asked 'Have you, by any chance, a spare *Play for Today*, any length provided it's seventy-five or ninety?' What doesn't work is to approach, say, Dennis Potter with the suggestion he should write a play about the Boxer Rising, using only eight minutes of film. If you're lucky, Dennis will give the play that he has in him at that moment, and it won't be about the Boxer Rising.

Commission ten plays to get six; if your organisation is generous (and not looking over your shoulder) go for two to one. You may end up with an overabundance of good scripts, but that is hardly an embarrassment; they can always be used for your next strand.

The best writers are commissioned up to the hilt, and it may be months before your choice can start on your script. If he is working on a multi-episode serial, he will be out of circulation for many months; remembering the hazards of authorship, illness, or more frightening, that sudden drying up of inspiration, you would be unwise to offer him a commission unless you are very far ahead of production, and he would be mad to accept it. Television is not his only market. Every writer dreams of the big film for the cinema, and will turn the most tempting offer down if there is even the slimmest chance of it. There is also that sudden urge to drop everything and write a play for the theatre, which will almost certainly coincide with your commission.

If the producer cannot find one of his favourite writers free he must search out new talents. To help him, he will probably have a script editor, of his own choosing. Script editors are not a 'must', but for anything of a prolonged nature – a set of plays, series, serials – they are advisable. Many of them have been television writers, and their experience can be invaluable to the new producer (and the old).

The job description (to use a bit of establishment jargon) of the editor's job is deceptively straightforward. He or she will support the producer in the preparation and creation of his strand, by guiding him towards scripts and ideas with quality and viability, and in his search for new writing. When the writer is commissioned, the editor must make sure he understands the weight and scope of the work; it is pointless, and unkind, to allow a writer to rush off and create a film extravaganza, when his production is headed for a regional studio of laughable smallness. When the script is delivered, the editor must make sure that the brief has been carried out. Scripts have a way of growing, and nothing causes more chaos than a script commissioned at fifty minutes coming out at an optimistic eighty-seven.

The style of production is agreed on commissioning – an all-film, a tape-on-location, all or part studio. The writer can then work to the mode, and use its virtues.

Nothing starts without a script, and the sooner it is written and accepted, the better. Much of a script editor's life is spent in nagging overworked writers. In a long-running series, the editor has extra responsibilities, mainly of continuity. Once the main situations and characters are formed, the scripts must respect them. Most series have a number of writers, so the responsibility for literary continuity falls on to the editor. When a project is launched, he must compose a 'Bible' of the main characters, their professional backgrounds, their pasts, their relationships, habits, vices and strengths; plus at least an indication of any developments intended for them through the series – promotion, marriage, failure.

Both editor and producer will have to resist those colleagues (the directors, particularly) who try to bend the agreed conventions of the series, out of sheer boredom with sameness. After the first exhilarating months of *Z Cars* we, the directors, got tired of shooting the same three angles on the same small police station enquiry room. That's all there were – three: left, right and centre, unless one committed the supreme idiocy of having a camera in the ceiling to shoot the tops of everyone's heads. For one episode, I turned the entire enquiry room through ninety degrees, scrapping one wall, and putting a new one in. This put the familiar doors and windows in entirely different places, and the result was protests from disorientated viewers, and cries of reproof from the producer, David Rose.

The best part of the script editor's job is the encouragement of new writers; and having found them, helping them to get their first television scripts right. It takes patience to guide a bristling and talented young playwright with three fringe theatre successes behind him; it takes sheer gall to insist on further changes when he has just submitted his third rewrite. And an even more gossamer touch is needed with an experienced writer who has hit a tired and stale patch, and is behind with his deliveries, and his mortgage.

Writers, like actors, thrive under encouragement; if they have respect for an editor, they will listen to him. But it has to be admitted that many television writers bitterly resent the script editor, convinced that he stands between him and the producer/director; that his, the writer's, ideas are misrepresented, and probably mislaid. It boils down inevitably to cases: not just overbearing editors, but convinced or unconvinced writers.

Not all writers are as meticulous in research as they might be, and the responsibility of checking up on them will probably fall on the editor. This can range from double-checking the accuracy of a detailed experiment by Marie Curie, to matters more mundane. If, in the script, there is an unpleasant drug-taking barber called Spiniski living in Southwold, the editor must make certain there are no barbers (heroin addicts or not) with even remotely similar names living in Southwold. Even with this vigilance, the most disastrous coincidences occur, and then life is all solicitors' letters and grave consultations in Lincoln's Inn Chambers.

Script editors become specialists by association. The editor on *The Onedin Line*, the long-running BBC series about a Victorian shipping line, became an authority on bills of lading, star sights, rigging and

Victorian harbour regulations. The editor in *Colditz*, an expert on the paraphernalia of German prison camps and escapes.

Efficient editors are worth their weight in anything. They can make everyone's life easier, by cutting the literary corners and keeping a good relationship with the writers. It's hardly surprising that so many of them go on to become successful producers.

Drama making is a complicated occupation; a breakdown in any one of its stages can grind the whole machine to a standstill. A common cry from those who do not understand this is 'If only we could have early scripts, everything would be solved . . .' Everything? No one is arguing; and no one sets out deliberately to have late scripts.

The accidents that clutter the scriptual path are many. Apart from illness, a natural hazard, there is the writer's fatal error of allowing himself to be over-commissioned. A change of Channel Controller or Departmental Head can alter the composition of the year's work. Scripts may be disappointing, or fail altogether, resulting in hurried substitutions. The ideal is simple: 'All scripts in hand months before the production run-up'. Unfortunately scripts do not roll off the line like plastic cups, and the ideal is not so much unlikely as impossible. No one needs convincing that the late script is everyone's curse – it forces producers and directors into the second rate, simply because there is no time for anything else. Every script editor should have a plaque on his desk that reads 'commission early – if possible, a week before that'!

Mysteriously, despite all these fatal hazards, there is still an apparently endless flow of good television drama in this country, and it is one of its prime exports to the rest of the world.

Classic Plays

Classic is a woolly term. It embraces Euripides, Marlowe, Shakespeare, Restoration rollick, a Victorian melodrama, a Brechtian experience; it includes Conrad and Maugham, Galsworthy and Rattigan, O'Neil, O'Casey, Tennessee Williams and Arthur Miller; if it *has* a meaning, it is a play that has survived the test of time.

The producers of classics start with the bonus of world-proven plays, but there are traps, not the least of which is an over-anxiety to play homage to the great; a guilty feeling that 'My God, it's over three years since we did an Ibsen!' There is no logical case to be made for annual Ibsens, or annual anything else. Any classic television play output will certainly be modest, and it must therefore be intelligently selective, neither aggressively antique, nor self-consciously twentieth century. An earnest season of northern European drama drawn from the works of Strindberg, Brecht and Ibsen, would be better lightened with a little Shaw or Wilde. There is in some quarters the same snobbery about classic plays as there is about vintage cars; nothing counts unless it is over fifty years old. There are modern classics in plenty – Pinter's *The Caretaker*, Osborne's *The Entertainer*, Miller's *The Crucible*, Rattigan's *The Browning Version*, a short play, but one of his finest.

Another trap is an over-reverence for the dead author's work, a conviction that every word must be sacrosanct. It isn't. There are few perfect plays; most are improved by a little cutting, some by a lot. I have yet to enjoy heartily a full-length version of *Hamlet* or *Tamburlaine*, and the three parts of Shakespeare's *Henry VI* need vigorous pruning if they are to be enjoyable. No one should shrink from cutting great plays; their dead authors would probably, with hindsight, have done the same.

Theatre plays are often confined by old unities and conventions to one or two interior sets. No producer should spread their backgrounds, just for the sake of it, but television drama usually benefits by it. Houses have gardens and upstairs rooms, courtrooms have corridors and private chambers. It is sometimes rewarding to see the Judge before he enters the court.

Series and Serials

Their production problems derive from their form, and the time-span they cover. Series proper, like *Angels*, *Shoestring*, *Minder*, are usually written by a harmonious team of writers; the great novels, however, must be adapted by one writer only; it is artistic lunacy to split *Anna Karenina* between a team. The twenty episodes of *War and Peace* were dramatised by the late Jack Pulman, who also did the whole of *I, Claudius*; Simon Raven adapted the twenty-six episodes of the Trollope's *Palliser* novels. These dramatisations are artistic plums, demanding a particular skill, and the experts will have to be commissioned as far as two years ahead of production.

The formalities of television management do not favour this

long-sightedness. Cautious channel controllers are nervous of committing so much screen time so far ahead on a project that is no more than a blank page and a promise to fill it; especially as the whole enterprise may go flat on its face from its first transmission. Television's financial pundits, aware of the small fortunes involved, are glumly aware that once the juggernaut has been set rolling, there will be no stopping it.

Assume now optimistically, that the producer has commissioned the writer of his heart, that the scripts are being written and actually look like being delivered vaguely on time. This happy condition is no more than a starting point for the other logistics of preparation.

With the promise of scripts, directors can be approached, a production team assembled. Everyone has his favourite designer, studio crew, technical manager, his star film-cameraman, his only possible costume designer; and there are producers who take it as a personal insult from management if any one of their choices is already working for someone else.

There is graphic design. Once this consisted of little more than plain opening and closing title sequences, and a mass of supplementary design within the drama – fascias of shops, special newspapers, authentic documents, signposts, names on doors. Then title sequences (as in the cinema) began to have a life and energy of their own; specially filmed for series like *Angels* or *The Onedin Line*; often brilliantly simple like the Russian dolls for *Tinker, Tailor, Soldier, Spy*. Sometimes the least complicated graphic design is the most effective, as for example, *Secret Army*, the war-time series about the Belgian Resistance.

The title sequences for this were designed by Alan Jeapes. Both opening and closing sequences were based on still photographs taken in Belgium and France. The opening sequence created an impression of an aircrew member parachuting from his stricken aircraft, and making his way to a safe house. This was done by a 'pan down' from a moonlit sky to a farmhouse, then tracking on a series of stills, using the subjective camera technique, to finish up at the safe house – indicated by a lighted window at the end of a village street. This, the opening title sequence, indicated *arrival*.

The end titles, using the same technique, tracked *out* from a series of stills of French roads and railway lines, through mountains to the sea. This symbolised the travels of an escaper conducted through France, over the Pyrenees into Spain, his eventual arrival at the Mediterranean and the final escape back to England.

The music was composed by Robert Farnon, matching precisely and artistically the visual 'story' worked out by the graphic designer. For these titles Alan Jeapes, in 1979, received two major graphic design awards.

A good graphic sequence, with compelling music over it, can actually sell a show to a viewer wavering between one channel and another; and the music can bring him in from the garden. The same composer will probably (though not necessarily) provide the incidental music to be used within the production – often a series of variations on the main theme. Composers today expect to work to an edited tape or film, so that their music will *fit*, technically and emotionally.

Casting, of which a lot more in the next chapter, is a split responsibility. No producer can avoid his own preferences – the mere reading of a script immediately conjures up the ideal actors and actresses. On the other hand, no director of quality likes to have a complete cast handed to him on arrival, as a *fait accompli*.

It is largely a horses-for-courses matter. For the single play, provided the director is called in early enough, casting is a matter for discussion between producer and director; but the director should insist on his own choices.

Those classics or adaptations where only one director is involved should come into the same category – director and producer in double harness, if not always in single harmony.

For the long-running series – *All Creatures Great and Small*, *Angels* – which spread over years and may employ a dozen directors *en route*, the producer must have the right to cast the permanent characters. He will be working with them long after the directors have gone off to make feature films in Herne Bay and Hong Kong.

As the director has now arrived, we can move on to his role.

7

The Director: Preparation

Whatever the medium, however large the budget or small the theatre, the director has the best job in drama. The writer and actor are close behind, particularly when they are successful. But to the director falls the final welding of the talents; only he can unite the skills surrounding the production – script, cast, background – and give them their full corporate value. By the same token, he can bring the whole enterprise to ruin, by imcompetence and insensitivity.

For this view of television, I am assuming that we are working with the best, for that is what we all desire. The best directors are aristocrats, beloved (or at least respected) by those who work with them. Artists refer with affection to a director as being 'an actor's director', and this is a professional compliment. It means one who understands the actor's problems, disperses them, and guides him to a better performance than he thought himself capable of. Many such directors have been actors themselves for a while, and have not forgotten how depressing it can be.

Acting can be a joy or a torment. When you are good in a part – in a comedy role with a packed house falling about laughing at your every 'Pass the salt, Mabel' – there is little better in the world. When you are mediocre in a part, and know it, and worst of all, seem unable to improve it, this is the moment for the confidence generated by the actor's director; he is not only sure you can be superb in the part, but actually shows you how to be quite good. There are not many actors and actresses who can resist such help; those who do, through arrogance or insensitivity, are rarely worth fostering.

Drama direction is about scripts, and about actors. In television the director is chosen by the producer. But the best directors choose themselves, in that they will only do the scripts that attract them, a piece of autocracy that rouses surprisingly little resentment in a competitive profession.

Drama is a very personal profession. Writers form close liaisons with producers, directors with actors, with designers, film cameramen and actors. These relationships are jealously guarded, and the outrage of a director who has been told that his favourite cameraman is not available has to be seen to be believed. Useless to explain that the cameraman in question will be filming for someone else on the Great Wall of China for the next six months. The director wants him and no one else, and will somebody kindly arrange it?

For five years, as a television writer/director, I wrote my own scripts for a company of actors, many of whom had been with me in the theatre. I wrote *for* them – tailor-made parts for each; and if I was sometimes accused of running an exclusive dramatic club, it was at least a good one, with distinguished members like Patrick Cargill, Gwendoline Watford, Joan Sanderson, Colin Douglas, Barry Letts and Francis Matthews.

The top director must be wooed with a top script; he will rarely make blind dates. Only a proven relationship between him, the writer and the producer, confirmed by success, will allow him to take it for granted that the next script will be as good as the last. The director is a freelance; he can reasonably argue that his next play, series or serial, may take a year of his professional life. If the result is disaster it will dog him for as long again. With a completed script in the hand, everyone knows the score.

The script that cannot be improved has yet to be written. If Shakespeare were writing for television today, he would be asked for rewrites, especially for *Titus Andronicus* and *Two Gentlemen of Verona*. The director may admire the writer extravagantly, and remain convinced that he has not yet got his script right – the bones are these, but wrongly arranged. On the other hand, he may find gold in the script unsuspected by the writer himself, which is good luck for the writer, if secretly disconcerting.

Few producers are charitable enough to suppress a spurt of irritation, when the director joining the production airily informs him that the script that he (the producer) has been nursing to perfection for months is less than perfect. But the wise producer bites on the bullet, and harkens. After all, when did he ever meet a reasonable director, who did not want to alter/improve/reshape/shorten/lengthen any script put before him? But that director, like that script, was his choice, and he presumably has some regard for his opinions. Only the director can see his personal end-product, enriched into three dimensions. Change the director, you will get a different end-product, but it will still be a director's vision.

There are degrees of acceptance or rejection. If a director hates a script, he has no problem – he refuses it; and the rare, perfect scripts allow no argument. It is the cases in between that are difficult, where the director can see the potential, and knows that it has only been partially realised. Discussion between writer and director can mend this. The weary writer, having had his third (and, surely, *last*) rewrite accepted by the producer, will not be enraptured by a string of new suggestions. But the director may have spotted the fatal flaw – his eye is fresh to the work – and everyone will finally be grateful.

He may also have missed the point completely, and be talking arrant nonsense. It is then up to the experienced producer and script editor to recognise this, and take evading action.

There are no set rules for mutual respect. It can be long-standing, hard won, or excitingly spontaneous. Drama is a profession of extremes, and its attachments tend to be full-blooded.

Directing should be a pleasure. But before it can be, the director must establish his credentials, and not only with his cast. Facing the unproven director will be doubting cameramen, sceptical designers, and overworked composers, all waiting to be convinced.

What they recognise, and welcome, is a climate of decision and confidence. There is no more pleasant surprise for those who service television than the director who actually knows what he is talking about, and is not going to make it up as he goes along.

Directors must be as self-engrossed as painters and sculptors, devoted, for the period of production, to the creation of a single item, merging the willing talents *en route*. The producers control a whole strand – a dozen plays, a set of classic adaptations. The director, whilst paying polite attention to the general output, is more intent on proving that his *Hamlet* will contain things that would surprise Shakespeare himself; or, on a lower plane, that his eight hundredth episode of that imperishable soap opera *Jubilee Terrace* will make the other seven hundred and ninety-nine look like a warm-up.

Television drama usually allows the director a generous preparation time. In an ideal world, he would work with writer/producer/script editor from the moment of inception, but television's appetite and turn-over make this a pipe-dream rarely experienced.

Assume then that the script is buoyant. The director has made his points, writer and producer have conceded them; the writer has taken himself off in reasonable heart for this last lap. The producer has already booked certain essential facilities – rehearsal room, studio space, recording and editing time, resources for pre-filming. By the time the director arrives he will probably have secured other specialists – the designer, costume, make-up, the lighting technical manager and so on, all of whom the director must accept.

The urgent priority is to cast the drama. There are over 20,000 actors and actresses in Britain. The ones you want will almost certainly be busy when you need them. Television is the largest employer of acting talent in drama's history – literally thousands of parts are cast every year. Logically this should mean work for everyone. In fact, it means constant work for some, intermittent work for many, and strong competition for the stars, whose only problem is deciding which plum to pick.

Actors in television, like zoologists and antique experts and quiz-masters, are always in danger of becoming the 'flavour of the year'; no screen is complete without them, and only early casting will trap them. Nor will your second and third choices be much less elusive. But beating down the director's door are impatient costume designers eager to fit actors for costumes, before passing them down the line to be measured for wigs. Without actors, none of it can begin. So who does the casting in television drama? I admit to a prejudice, seeded in the theatre, that casting is the privilege of the director. He, in the end, is the one who will have to cope with the cast, chide and cheer them, and bring their performances to the boil at the right moment. But television has its own circumstances and there are times when the director must forgo this privilege. If, for example, he joins a long-running series – *Coronation Street* or *Angels* or *Juliet Bravo* – he will find his permanent characters waiting for him, secure in their success and suspicious of change.

He may not admire their performances, but he would do well to conceal this, as he will still have to work with them. The rest of the cast, the supporting characters in that particular episode, must be his to cast. In the long-running series, the trick is to 'cast up' these parts as strongly as possible. Actors, after long months in a series, are often tempted, perhaps unconsciously, to rest on their laurels, to freewheel. Their performances and attitudes are set, and they are happy to cruise along unless challenged. Nothing is better for them than strong opposition from the supporting parts. The suspicion that a superior performance is stealing one's scene is an extraordinary spur to one's enthusiasm.

Yet even for this subsidiary casting, the producer may hover, anxiously. It is part of his job to make sure that the same popular, easily recognised artistes do not reappear week after week, in very different parts, thus confounding the reality of the series. It is disconcerting for the viewer when last week's Methodist minister turns up in the next episode as a rapist. Though I suppose anything is possible nowadays.

Casting the single play is another world. They are individual, separate, and their casting is entirely the director's affair. The producer has almost certainly lived longer with the script, but once casting begins, he and the director start equal. But the director *must* choose his own actors; he has to work with them. Later he can console himself ruefully that if the production is a success, everyone will congratulate the producer; if it turns out to be a 'dog', the director will be in the doghouse. But whether the play ends in delight or disaster will have much to do with the skill with which it has been cast.

What is true for the single play must be true for *any* project that has one director: a serial adaptation of a classic or modern novel is no more than an elongated play and, as such, is a single casting responsibility.

The director who has come up through the profession – from the theatre, or as a TV assistant – will know actors. But how, if you had landed from Mars (and somewhat surprisingly been snapped up to direct the newest Dennis Potter play) would you set about casting?

The director is not without allies. He has a producer presumably who is sympathetic and probably more experienced. He has a writer, who may have conceived the script with certain artistes in mind. In some organisations, he may have a casting director. He has assistants. As a last resort he has a departmental Head, who has been through the same mill in his time. Unfortunately, establishment figures, however practically experienced, are suspect, and their most exciting casting suggestions are usually received with polite reserve. How many times, to my dismay, have I seen that wary look on the faces of directors and producers, which says '*Now* what am I being sold? I mean, what's this with Peggy Ashcroft?' If these multiple advisers are not enough, there are auditions, the traditional theatrical way of finding new talent; more necessary, perhaps, for the juveniles, than for the leads and character parts.

Auditions should be personal and practical, a way of getting close to new, and usually nervous, talents. In my early theatre days, before the Second World War, the great managements used to hold General Auditions, open to all. The word would run up St Martin's Lane and down Shaftesbury Avenue that *they* were auditioning the Henry James thing at the Globe Theatre. Everyone would turn up in his best clothes (or someone else's – there was a lot of borrowing) and each would have his turn on the dimly lit stage.

Halfway back in the stalls would be a huddled group, who would use your audition as an opportunity for loud muttering. Most of these occasions ended with the cold, formal phrase: 'Thank you, Mr-?er- we'll let you know', and that was the end of that, because they didn't.

I still wonder what was the point in such general mêlées. The managements were casting important new plays – they had the pick of the profession to choose from. Were any of those eager young actors who walked out on to those dark stages ever cast? Or were the auditions just for conscience's sake, to keep the threatening mob quiet?

Auditions should be selective, the actors called by name and by invitation. There will be no difficulty in arranging them. Just let it be known that you are searching for a short twenty-year-old blonde with a Durham accent, and your office will fill with giant brunettes, whose accents range from Aberdeen to Aberystwyth; the optimistic theory being that you will be so taken by their readings that you will have the script completely rewritten to suit them.

Happily, serious agents know better, and send what you ask for. Audition sparingly. Do not try to see too many in one day; they will all merge together, and it is bad luck on the last two in. Talk to the actors first – most of them will be nervous. If you can, give them the chance to be alone with the script for a while. If their reading is anything near what you want, ask them to read again. They're usually better the second time.

There is a wry story about a not very good actor who for years went to all the auditions, but was never cast. One day, after a reading, he was stunned to be offered an excellent part. 'No, no,' he protested. 'I only do auditions.'

New directors are sometimes wary of asking experienced actors to read for them. But everyone wants to work, and courtesy covers all. It is good manners for the director to have done a little home-work on his auditionees; to know, for example, what drama they have done recently. There have been famous gaffes. One very young director invited an extremely eminent old actress to his office for a reading. Faced by this formidable lady, he became very nervous and blurted out: 'Now, Miss S., what exactly have you done?' The actress twinkled at him, secure in her two columns in *Who's Who in the Theatre*. 'You mean, this morning?' she said kindly.

Excellent actors may read very badly. Leslie Phillips, that most fluent of comedians, with a gossamer touch with lines, could not, as a young actor, string two sentences together at a first reading without stumbling. On the other hand, a lively audition does not guarantee a quality performance. There are professional auditionees – breezy, fluent, confident, full of hidden promise of better to come. The trouble is, there isn't. You have had it all at the audition, and it usually gets worse, not better.

Video cassettes have caused a quiet revolution in casting. Most television drama ends up, officially or otherwise, on cassettes. As they can be run back, and played again and again, they make perfect auditions.

Lastly, there is the grapevine. Drama people talk of little other than drama, and are generous in helping each other; provided, of course, they are not after the same part themselves. Theatrical pubs and clubs are full of directors eager to give advice. When I was stumped for casting in television, I would walk out of my office and shout 'Who could play Shylock?' Doors would open all down the passage, and by the time I'd got back to the safety of my office I would have more than my pound of flesh of Shylocks; at least one of which might be a good idea.

There are scores of theatrical agents, ranging from the great establishments with their strings of stars, to the modest newcomer with a dozen unknowns. The great artists do not need agents to *find* work for them; they need them for negotiation and for advice on choice. The theatrical agent is a stock figure of satire – he is the man who reluctantly allows his client 90 per cent of his earnings. There are bad agents, who do their clients more harm than good. There are excellent ones – personal representatives – who form long friendships with their artists, protect and guide their careers, even lend them money to keep going. Agencies establish their own credentials, and the less scrupulous are quickly known. The good ones are invaluable to casting, and should be heeded.

Television cannot match the fees offered for feature films, but casting should always be ambitious. No director should say, 'Oh it's no good asking Alec Guinness – he'd never do it.' He might; he might have been yearning to play that particular character for years.

Tempt him with scripts. Once you have even a half-promise of his agreement, your parsimonious management will mysteriously find the money for him.

Casting requires patience; it is a waiting game of wheedling and face-saving compromise. Television exempts the director from the sordid matter of discussing money with artists; this is done by a corps of 'bookers', office troglodytes locked in permanent argument with artists and agents, ranging from the passionate (scornful rejection of the insulting pittance offered to his client) to the practical rearrangement of filming or rehearsal dates.

Agents are usually reluctant to commit their artists too far in advance, fearful that they might miss that major feature film to be shot in Tierra Del Fuego, or the long-awaited call to play King Lear at the National Theatre.

The 'run-up' preparation time in TV drama has steadily increased, an expansion first generated by the arrival of full colour, and annually augmented by new complexities. The sophisticating of television drama has not been confined to writers and directors; their ambitions have been shared by designers of sets and costumes and make-ups, of lighting and cameramen and other skills. Those who 'service' drama are no longer content to be mere suppliers of background, of acres of wood and canvas, stock costumes and wigs refurbished for the twentieth time. To meet these ambitions, preparation 'run-up' time has swollen mightily, allowing the specialists to get alongside the director as soon as possible after his arrival. He will not have to seek them out; they will be lined up outside his office, script in one hand, plans and sketches in the other. As the casting is now under weigh, he can safely invite in the first of them – the set designer.

The Set Designer

The set designer is a specialist in two directions – artistic and practical. He must have a knowledge of materials and their use, of paint and plastic, colours and hues. He must understand draughtsmanship and proportion, how long the processes of TV design take and what they cost. He must combine the traditional dramatic crafts with the latest electronic novelties. He should be *au fait* with the shape of Elizabethan kitchens, Georgian staircases, the pattern of Roman floors, Regency wallpapers, Renaissance mirrors and Restoration beds. Nor is this rich knowledge enough in itself; he must be able to convert it dramatically. Without a sense of theatre he is nothing; his art is the old one of sham and fine deception. The best designers are cunning fakers.

He will have read the script, recognised the period in which it is set, its characters and their position in the story, the characters' taste or lack of it, what their money would buy and what they would want to buy with it. Social myths and customs change by the generation; if the script is historical, the designer must appreciate the social standing of the people in it, relative to the rest of their world.

The characters must *live* in their sets. They must be credible, not only in size and shape, but in the practicalities of property. The doors must close convincingly, the curtains pull, the taps gush and the gasfires pop. Cupboards and desks must be filled with the bric-à-brac of life, things must look used. It is easy to give a room a rich and sparkling look in colour television; it is much harder to make it look lived in and shabby.

This is only a corner of the designer's responsibility. With his team, he is responsible for everything that the viewer sees, and quite a lot that he does not. He will supply background and style, real or fantastic, dressed with mundane or magic properties. He will conjure it up, by some professional sleight of hand, accurately and on time, in studio or on location.

Television drama is an operation planned with optimism, and is consequently often forced behind schedule. To achieve an end product at all is a strain on nerves and energy – to do it *well* is exhausting. Hardly surprising then that it is full of professional partnerships which cut corners and misunderstandings and streamline the production strains. Not the least of these liaisons is that between director and designer.

Television successes are spectacular, saluted by millions; its disasters are equally public. Theatre plays die unnoticed in their empty theatres, while very bad films do not get a national showing. But a television 'dog' must have its day. A thirteen-part series will be three-quarters recorded before the first episode hits the screen. However bad its reputation, it takes a courageous television magnate to scrap the other twelve episodes. Anything that reduces the chance of such disasters – and the talented partnership of two minds and two pairs of eyes is one such thing – is a step on the way.

The designer will arrive in a flutter of plans and sketches. If the play is to be studio-recorded, his ideas will relate to that mode; if an all-film, he will have formed his own images of the locations – towns and factories, streets, shops, viaducts, rivers. For the all-film he can do little until these locations are firm; when they are finalised they will still not be perfect and it is a matter of how much or how little he will need to do to them.

Let us assume that the play is set in the rural England of 1769. The principal locations are a Queen Anne manor, with certain out-buildings; an eighteenth-century street in a small market town; a Norman church with a churchyard and a lych gate; a mill with a waterwheel. Ideally, all these locations would be close to each other, so that the unit can settle down comfortably in a convenient hotel, and saunter along each morning to the location of the day. In reality, the manor will be in Oxfordshire, the village street in Suffolk, the Norman church in Berkshire and the mill in Buckinghamshire on the edge of the glider club airfield. This adds considerably to the cost of the production, as the whole unit will constantly be moving from hotel to hotel; it only needs a few days of rain to throw the whole delicate structure into chaos.

The locations have been settled. The owners of the Queen Anne manor have lunatically agreed to allow a horde of people to invade their beautiful home, score the polished floors, spill coffee down the Chinese wallpaper, and make the early hours of the morning hideous with unruly crowd scenes.

The designer will arrive with a list of demands, divided into additions and conversions. He will ask to build an imposing gate house at the end of their drive, to be stormed by angry peasants, a folly in the meadow and, in the field behind the house, a thatched barn to be burnt to the ground by the mob. By way of conversion he will wish to take away the television aerial, remove all the curtains from the windows, obscure any modern additions with false shrubs and trees, and fit a new front door. Subsequently he will ask the vicar of the Norman church if he can add seven tombstones and an open grave to his collection. The owner of the mill will have an electrically operated waterwheel added to his decrepit property, and the eighteenth-century street will be transformed by new names over the shops, an ancient oak to mask off the telephone box, and acres of plastic cobbles.

The incredible patience of the British, rooted in a sort of despairing humour, allows them to accept these invasions; an acceptance some-time made easier by the large facility fees paid for their trouble.

For the modern play, the conversion may be less extreme. But even those locations which contain all the right features always have them in the wrong relative positions. The telephone box is not outside the bank, as demanded by the script, but on an island in the middle of teeming traffic; the pillar box is the wrong shape, and the bus-stop is the wrong sort.

Bizarre accidents occur. I once set up a false pillar box in a side street and was all set to film round it when an elderly lady came along and posted three letters in it. We had the greatest difficulty explaining her error to her, and only finally convinced her by lifting the pillar box off the ground and showing her her three letters lying on the pavement. She then got extremely angry (it is a British trait to get cross when embarrassed) and accused us of sharp practices in robbing the Royal Mail.

These conversions are routine to the designer; he would probably be uneasy if he found a location perfect in every detail.

If the drama is part-film, part-studio, with only certain sequences on film (as with most TV drama), the designer will have the additional problem of matching film to studio. A character must not open a blue door on film and close a yellow one in the studio. The neat little semi-detached house, with an elegant bow window, must not turn into a mini mansion with stern oblong casements inside; and, obviously, such glaring mistakes are not made. But even the mildest error produces cross letters from lynx-eyed viewers to the Director General, demanding to know why the licence money is being so flagrantly misused in this manner.

Television design has to stand daily comparison with the opulence of feature films. Viewers are often unaware whether they are looking at a 'bought-in' film or a domestically made drama, and they expect the same gloss on both. As feature films have always insisted on an absolute reality of background, that is what a great proportion of the viewers expect from television drama.

Stylisation works well in the theatre. The whole ambience is theatrical, artificial – rows of people in a formal playhouse, sharing an occasion that is obviously non-real. The scenery may be as close to reality as the theatre can manage, but it is still obviously scenery. The ingenious composite sets for such giant musicals as *Oliver*, *Evita* and *Sweeney Todd* are as much marvels of engineering as stage design; magnificent, exciting, original, but it is not *real*.

Television has made its own attempts at stylisation, with mixed success. *The Devil's Crown*, the long BBC Serial about the first three Plantagenet kings – Henry II, Richard I, and John made no pretence at background reality. Arches were truncated at the top, walls ended in mid-air, gardens were fantastical. The performances and the direction were excellent, but the public remained uneasy. The obvious unreality of the design confused them; and one not very bright television journalist wrote that this was yet one more aspect of BBC poverty – we could no longer afford to finish the sets. More successful was a trilogy of plays by Ian Curteis about Orde Wingate, the eccentric Second World War general. The setting for this was stylised to the point of being no more than a collection of giant blocks, ingeniously lit, and punctuated by monochrome clips from official war films. So extreme was the stylisation that it was more readily accepted by the viewers than the half-stylisation of *The Devil's Crown*. More recently, Jonathan Miller, producing the third and fourth year's output of the BBC's Shakespeare Canon, developed a style that he had already experimented with some years before in his production of *King Lear*. He reduced background scenery to a vivid minimum. Its style echoed great painters that he admired – Veronese for *Antony and Cleopatra*, Turner for *The Merchant of Venice*, the seventeenth-century Dutch and Flemish masters for *All's Well That Ends Well*. He used light in a way that was almost tangible, and brought his artists to the foreground. He made Shakespeare in television exactly what it should be – fine actors delivering lines of genius in conditions of absolute clarity.

Electronic 'aids' to production are increasingly used in drama. Colour Separation (which, broadly speaking, is the electronic insertion of a moving or still background *separately* behind the performers and the more solid foreground parts of the settings) has been widely used for the more fantastic programmes, science fictions like *Dr Who* or *Blake's Seven*, semi cartoon plays like *Alice Through the Looking-Glass*, Tommy Steele's *Quincey*; and for more serious plays like Voltaire's *Candide*; more recently by Philip Saville – a skilled user of electronic trickery – in *The Ghost Sonata* and *The Journal of Bridget Hitler*.

Colour Separation's more sophisticated cousin Quantel (it has other names) is considerably more flexible and time saving, and can produce almost any visual fantasy, splitting and quartering the screen, moving images in any direction, controlling their sizes and development. The only reservation I have about such marvels is that they can be so visually arresting that they overcome the play itself; which, to me, is a step in the wrong direction. If, in a theatre, I find myself admiring the scenery for too long, the play itself is not holding me. In television, the visuals can be so powerful that they literally force themselves on the viewer's attention, to the exclusion of all else. The answer, of course, is to use such aids for productions that actually *need* them (and to use them with balance) so that they do not become the play itself. Stylisation cannot be logically extended to a lot of television drama – the crime and hospital series, the soap operas, the dramatisations of the great novels. But there is a lot to be done yet with electronic backgrounds.

First meetings between director and designer should be brisk and practical. 'The kitchen should be smaller, they must be falling over each other . . .' or 'he couldn't afford a house this size – he's a bank clerk in the thirties . . .'

Between old colleagues, the criticisms can be more picturesque; 'Marvellous Adam staircase, Tony. I love the way it sweeps majestically round the back of the entire set, and descends in a radiant curve to the pillared hall below. But the bloody scene only lasts twelve seconds. Why can't Arthur kiss Alice in the library?'

Settings must be logical. The rooms must not exist in limbo – their windows must look out on what one expects the view to be; the fireplace should at least suggest that it connects with the noble chimneys seen in the filming, rather than to the modest gas connection in the studio wall. Corridors and kitchens, barns and bedrooms must be the right size; at the same time cameras and microphones must be able to do their work of seeing and hearing actors. Lighting, too, must have physical access to illuminate the sets.

The designer should offer all sorts of dramatic features – different levels, odd corners, angles, foreground objects, decorations; what he should avoid are intricate (and expensive) features that will never be seen by the cameras. As with the actors, the talents must be plainly in the shop window.

The best designers superimpose their own signature style; one does not have to wait for the end captions to say Eileen Diss, or Sally Hulke, or David Myerscough-Jones, Tony Abbott, Colin Lowrey, Tim Harvey . . .

Practical points agreed, the designer starts the process that ends with a collection of sets in a studio. Today's television design matches the best of cinema, at a fraction of the cost. Most drama sets are built from scratch; there is little revamping of old stock. The computer has assured us (and who would dare to challenge it?) that it is more economical to destroy scenery after use, rather than store it. Most of it is cannibalised, taken apart, or just destroyed. So eager are these agents of destruction, the designer must be rapid in putting his mark on any sets required for subsequent episodes.

How different from the simple fifties when, as a writer/director, I used to wander round the studios before writing my next episode, to see what rich scenery might be going free a few weeks ahead. Having put my mark on a riverside wharf, George II's aviary, a Regency ballroom (corner of) and a corridor in Brighton Pavilion, I would dash off an historical episode with these opulent backgrounds. There was no difficulty in acquiring sets in this unofficial way; it was actually easier than asking for 'three more feet on the left wall of the sitting room', a request that always caused a grave controversy about 'man hours'. One rarely got one's 'three more feet on the left wall'; what one got was a curtain over an imaginary window, always inexplicably drawn against the hot June day outside.

In those days the designer cowered, and still does, under the tyranny of the 'man hour'. Let no one think that a 'man-hour' is the amount of work a man can do in an hour. It is a complex unit of measurement, relating to the construction, painting and movement of items of scenery; its cost is staggering.

This light-hearted view of one of the BBC's sacred cows led me into trouble in my early days with Children's Television Drama. The Head of the department was a splendid lady called Freda Lingstrom, who had invented (with Maria Bird) many nationally famous puppets, like Andy Pandy, the Woodentops, the Flowerpot Men. She was a very correct, sometimes severe administrator, a stern critic of everything one did, but a stout supporter when things went wrong. She kept an eagle eye on violence, and, as far as she was concerned, sex was a number between five and seven. She held a weekly meeting with her directors, to make sure no one was getting out of hand, and at one of these meetings announced, somewhat coyly, that none of us should ask for the services of Miss Eileen Diss (television's prettiest designer) as *Miss* Diss was going to have a baby. In the respectful silence that followed, I said how glad I was that one designer at least had had enough man hours. After a brief and scandalised pause, whilst this regrettable penny dropped, I was asked to leave the meeting. I suppose I was lucky not to be asked to leave the building, and decent society.

The BBC's moral tone has always been a little sterner than the national average. There have been famous disgraces. In the pre-war days of sound broadcasting, before television arrived to rock the decencies, a programme announcer was surprised in his office, embracing a girl robustly. He was immediately sent home in disgrace

– 'suspended'. The man's friends rallied and assured the Director-General, a moral martinet, that the object of the man's unbridled passion was in fact his fiancée who was due to become his wife in a matter of days. Authority thawed slightly. The Director-General sent a message to say that the man could be restored to the permanent staff, but that he must *never read the Sunday Lesson again*. If that isn't true, it ought to be.

The designer, with his assistants, now prepares a series of plans and elevations of the sets, detailed to the point that they can be contracted by staff with no knowledge of the scripts.

We clutter our lives with possessions. I dread the day when I shall have to move and be forced to empty the over-stuffed cupboards of the years. Television drama reflects the acquisitiveness of humans. Attached to every drama is a list of Properties (the old theatrical word for everything that is used or seen in a drama from a fully practical steam roller to a fourteenth-century Polish icon). Lists are extracted from the scripts and sent to the Property Buyer. He or she is another specialist. Property buying is more than knowing where to find a Victorian chaise-longue, and for how much. The buyer must have a working knowledge of history, of periods, of social customs. Like script editors, many of them have become experts perforce through the dramas they supplied. Those who worked on *The Duchess of Duke Street* became very knowledgeable in Edwardiana; those on the series *Secret Army* in German war-time documents, Belgian Resistance forgeries, and all the minutiae of life under enemy occupation.

Every year millions of articles move through the television studios and locations. The range is infinite – period vehicles, medieval weapons, Canadian log stoves, Chinese parchments, Russian samovars, Regency snuff boxes, Art Nouveau. Apart from those articles actually handled by the cast, each set must be dressed; there must be clocks and curtains, mirrors and door handles, stair carpets and oil lamps. Banquets must be provided (double rations, please, in case of retakes) and farmyards stocked. Every week, in *All Creatures Great and Small*, a complete veterinary surgery of the 1930s had to be set up in full detail. Hundreds of such sets are dressed each year, a miracle taken for granted, only noticed when it goes wrong.

It *does* go wrong, as I have known to my cost. All theatrical anecdotes are tales of disaster; the most common in the theatre is the gun that refuses to fire, leaving the actor to think up some other way of murdering his fellow actor. The most desperate of these stories concerns the panicking actor who, having clicked his revolver three times, rushed round behind his patient victim and kicked him robustly. His fellow actor, backing up traditionally, sank to his knees, whispering with his last breath 'The boot was poisoned . . .'

Now that television drama is all recorded, such laughable mishaps can be ironed out by retakes. In live television there was no such escape route. One comedy playlet I wrote gave rise to a major property confusion.

There was a purportedly funny scene in this play, when the hero is locked in the dungeon of a castle which is on fire. The jailer comes slowly down the steps to the cell door, smoke billowing round him, carrying a huge bunch of rusty keys. As tension and the flames rose, he had to try key after key in the lock, with no apparent urgency, to release the hero. To assist this comic *auto-da-fé*, I had indented on the Property List for 'fifty old keys, some very large, some smaller'.

On transmission day, I rode confidently up in the lift to Studio E at Lime Grove. When I got out I was confronted by a long vista of barrels. This continued into the studio itself. Every set was filled with barrels of varying sizes. In the centre of the studio, cameras and booms huddled together in the only space left by the invasion. 'What in the name of God are all these barrels?' I said testily. The property man was aggrieved. He handed me a list on which I read to my dismay 'Fifty old *kegs*, some very large, some smaller.' Kegs. Barrels, large and small, faithfully supplied. The only missing item was the fifty keys.

There were less dramatic impasses, as when my secretary asked for a forty-five-inch gun. Property responded courteously that the biggest gun they could find was a sixteen-inch, and this was attached to a battleship. Would a point four five do, to go on with?

Meanwhile, the director has had his attention seized by – the costume designer.

The Costume Designer

No one can design costumes without taste and flair, and no one should be rash enough to try without a hard knowledge of costume history and materials; of the social and sexual influence on costume; of the periodic changes dictated by vanity, common sense, or sheer commerce; even, in richer circles, by the taste of a Marie Antoinette or a Prince Regent. Only in recent years have the rigid links between social position and dress been eroded. Nowadays, given the trend prevailing, anyone from any walk of life can wear anything. There are few formal occasions left, like Ascot, the domain of the heavy in purse or the long in lineage. In my youth, dinner jackets were worn on first nights, and BBC radio announcers changed into them for their unseen evening broadcasts. As a stage director at a West End theatre, I wore a dinner jacket.

For many years television has abounded in series about the rich and the royal of history, sometimes giving an impression that even the less well off in those times were colourfully dressed. In truth, all periods have had their workaday clothes, and those for which we have photographic evidence suggest a considerable uniform shabbiness amongst all but the well-off. Prior to our present evened-out society, few people had much money for extra clothes, and even the rising middle classes tended to be crows rather than peacocks.

Costume designers are even greedier for information than set designers. Like the rest of the team they can only begin with the script and the characters; to which they will add their expert, sometimes acquired, knowledge of the period, its rules and snobberies. Their own taste and flair will supply a style for the production.

Pleasant discussion about style will be followed by a demand for useful facts. Which characters are in which episodes? Which are definitely in the pre-filming? On what dates? How old is Lucy Lymington? How rich is Sir John Flumpley? Has he any taste? Episode Five mentions casually that a large crowd of peasants bursts through the palace gates, burning, looting and killing. How large is this mob? Who do they kill? How many men, women? How closely will they be seen? Any close shots of the wounded, with blood?

The costume designer might at this point dismay the director by pointing out that although his story only moves through two and a half decades of history, there were within that period four radical changes of fashion. This was expensively true of *Prince Regent*, the BBC serial that followed the prince from youth to monarchy; many of the changes in style being generated by the clothes-conscious prince himself. The long Napoleonic Wars had cut off the supplies of exciting materials (especially from France) and after Waterloo, peace triggered off an exuberant explosion of opulent fashions. Much the same happened after the austerities of the Second World War, when the 'New Look' arrived.

The popularity of the long-running costume serials was sealed by the astonishing success of *The Forsyte Saga* in the late sixties. This twenty-six-parter became a 'must' with viewers everywhere, and the BBC repeated it to the point of exhaustion, while the National Film Theatre ran it as a twenty-four-hour marathon.

In its wake came a wave of period blockbusters – *The First Churchills*, *War and Peace*, *The Pallisers*, *Casanova*, *Edward the Seventh*, *Jennie*, *Lillie Langtry*, *Prince Regent*, *The Borgias*. They were immensely popular in America, where television viewers were starved of romantic drama. PBS, The Public Broadcasting Service in the States (as opposed to the three great national networks: ABC, NBC and CBS) serves relatively small areas in and around the great cities. Each of the three hundred local stations attempts to present better quality television – drama, ballet, music, documentaries. Unable to make enough of such dramas to fill their screens, they looked to British television. During the seventies, scores of British serials and series (even some single plays) found their way on to the PBS screens. So great was the invasion, it became an embarrassment, and a spur to objections from American guilds and unions. America has always been rich in playwrights, but particularly in the thirties, forties and fifties. Whatever its faults, Hollywood fathered films by the hundred and many of them were well written, often by those same major theatrical playwrights who had been seduced to the West Coast by irresistible offers. Little of their talents brushed off on to American television as it developed; after some valiant efforts by a few producers in the formative years, serious drama almost disappeared from the national networks. Routine series were the order of the day, predictable and action-packed, and it was left to the Public Broadcasting Service – notably New York, Boston and Los Angeles – to keep serious drama alive. Unable to afford enough of their own, they were quick to see the potential of buying British drama at very low prices.

This sudden eruption of period drama had its effect on the costume market. Suddenly, thousands more costumes were needed, from the age of King Arthur to the King Edward VII period. Most of the new television sagas covered several generations, and any character that survived had to be reclothed and reclothed again. Stocks were quickly exhausted, and specially made costumes became the norm. Where all these hundreds of costumes go to afterwards has always been something of a mystery. But it is a fact that anyone setting out to do yet another production of *Jane Eyre* will be told that there isn't a Victorian costume to be had, not even for television money.

They must all be made, particularly those for the three extras who will just pass through the back of the hall in Episode Five. The producer may protest that only a couple of years earlier three hundred Victorian costumes were made for *Mill on the Floss*, *Wuthering Heights* and *Nicholas Nickleby*. He will sternly be reminded that Super Mammoth Production Inc. are about to start filming their four-hour epic *Charles Dickens*, and have earmarked every Victorian costume from Lord Melbourne to Mafeking. Any attempt to clothe even a modest play about Disraeli will be frustrated by a Disraeli film being planned in Texas, Tripoli and Transylvania. There is not a frilled cravat to be had anywhere.

This means brand-new costumes, often costing more than the hard-working actors. The producer may protest; his objections will be carefully noted, and a committee will be set up to examine the matter in depth. The end product of these manoeuvres is the best dressed television drama in the world.

But the output is not all history and period opulence. Much of the costume designer's time will be taken up with policemen, army sergeants, bank clerks, barmaids, factory workers and managing directors; plus an army of extras and walk-ons who, though they may only inhabit the background of the picture, will certainly be picked out if they are wrongly dressed.

The richness of *Prince Regent* or *Jennie* is as great a treat for the costume designer as for the director or set designer. But, most of the work, for all of them, is less exciting, if no less necessary.

At this stage, the costume designer will ask for a full cast list. Useless to protest that it is still six weeks before the first rehearsal or location; that the agents are being more than usually tiresome about committing their actors, most of whom are filming in Bohemia. The designer's answer will be unrelenting; unless she has bodies, she cannot clothe them – unless, of course, the director will be content with a completely naked cast – a threat that seems to work quite often in the theatre. Having made herself plain, she will give way to – make-up.

Make-Up

Like her sister in Costume, she will have absorbed the script; even more like her she will be clamouring for actor's names. She will remind the director, as if it were the day's original thought, that she cannot begin without bodies, particularly heads. Apart from the usual discussion about period and social standing she will express an almost morbid interest in age and ageing. Television sagas tend to be what one American publicist regrettably described as 'a great and panoramic passing of the relentless years'. Translated, this means that the characters grow up, marry, have children, get old and watch their children making precisely the same mistakes as they did. Audiences enjoy this, particularly the children making the same mistakes.

The make-up artist will wish to know *how* these people age. Are they lined by crisis and disappointment, or have they retained their bloom. Attractive actresses will insist that they should indicate the passing of forty years by a distinguished silvering of the temples, and not a wrinkle anywhere. On the other hand the script may demand a degradation of Dorian Gray magnitude. Bones dictate the basic shape of our appearance, and it takes skill to impose the flabbiness of age on a finely sculptured face. In *I, Claudius*, Derek Jacobi had to change from elegant youth to the sagging flesh of age. Each week this had to be built up by hours of make-up, an ordeal cheerfully accepted by an actor provided the results are worth it.

Make-up is a most personal and intimate art. It can be portraiture in three dimensions. The actor has two assets, his talent and his looks, and he must put both in the shop window. His appearance matters, whether it is hideous or superb. Actors arrive at the make-up stage tensed up; it is the moment before they record their performances, and they are grateful for sympathy. A good make-up artist will see that his day starts well, sending him into the studio confident that he looks *right*.

Wigs, moustaches, false curls and toupees, postiche, are all part of the daily work. The domestic history of wigs is fascinating, bound up with social snobberies and conventions; the make-up artists must know them. In the theatre, make-ups are seen at a distance; and, like the occasion itself, may be recognisably theatrical. But in television, as in film, make-up must be totally convincing, standing up to pitiless close-ups. Artificial folds of flesh, bald domes, anywhere in fact where make-up joins the actual surfaces of face or neck, call for an exact skill, and for constant repair during the recording.

As with costume, much of it is workaday – straight make-ups, the addition of a moustache, a little greying of the hair. Like everything else in television, it has to be listed and costed and identified; in hundreds of cases, specially made, fitted, altered and fitted again.

Occasionally, make-ups of great intricacy (for example, *Jekyll and Hyde*) will be experimented with and checked on camera well before recording or filming.

Partly appeased by the names of those few actors who have thus far agreed to appear, the make-up artist will take herself off, leaving the director free to look for his script. There will be other visitors – the composer, to discuss the theme and incidental music; the graphic designer, for a last word on the title sequences; and, in some productions, visual effects.

Visual Effects

A department of dreamers, optimists, and skilled specialists; a somewhat solitary breed, engrossed in their own mysteries. In the early days of BBC television, these effects were dealt with almost entirely by two men – Jack Kine and Bernard Wilkie, aided by a team of rarely seen Georges and Charlies. Everything from the San Francisco earthquake to a talking carrot had to be discussed with one or other of this delightful and gentle pair. Only such super-mammoth epics as *Quatermass and the Pit* demanded the presence of both.

Jack and Bernard could make anything out of anything, at any time, and usually for five shillings. They would give you model houses, factories, villages, space stations, science fiction monsters, rockets, airships, ghosts and, above all, explosions. They loved explosions, from the London Blitz to an exploding cigar. They also liked comedy props and funny effects. They made me a flying pig, an Elizabethan invention to test the breaking strain of soldiers' helmets, a Regency diving bell, and a barge exploding in a French canal, taking with it a couple of unpleasing Gestapo officers. Their best, for me, was a full-sized medieval cannon that not only fired a cannon ball with real gunpowder, but was required to drop the ball out of the mouth of the cannon – and no further – on cue. This was live television, no second chance, no redress if they overdid the gunpowder and destroyed half the studio and any actors in the line of fire. It worked immaculately but I doubt if I would be allowed to do it today. There would be a *rule* about it.

Jack and Bernard were a remarkable pair; when one remembers that they did all the *Quatermass* effects *live*, one must salute their nerve even more than their skill. Visual Effects has now grown from an early family unit to a thriving part of drama production.

Casting has continued, compromises struck. Final setting plans have been pored over and accepted. There have been combined planning meetings, attended by all the contributing skills, including the chief lighting engineer (in BBC language the Technical Manager One), his colleague in charge of the recording and, if electronic effects are part of the production, the experts in that field. Difficulties have been identified and corrected. The team has been welded round the rehearsal script.

This script has been broken down into those sequences which must be shot on location – tape or film – and those that will be recorded in the studio. As most location work precedes the studio, we might as well do the same here.

8

The Director: Location

There is a romantic ring to the word filming. It recalls those vintage days when directors, virile in boots and breeches, hammered out the rules of film-making through megaphones. It suggests glittering locations in the capitals of the world, or well-regulated adventures in swamps and deserts. It hints at the company of compliant actresses, large cars, even larger fees. No one who works in television would recognise this romantic image, but a suspicion still lingers that those early film makers had a very good time.

The truth is that feature films were big business, and so prospered in the thirties. The cinemas emptied the provincial theatres, the repertories and the round-the-year tours. The films were primarily entertainment, but by no means rubbish. Many of them reflected the social problems of their day. The huge unemployment of the late twenties and early thirties generated serious films, and sparkling musicals abounded to take everyone's mind off their troubles. There were very funny comedies (that have never quite been matched) and, at all times, gangster movies. When the war came, the cinema changed gear to heroism and national sacrifice, and actors who couldn't blow the froth off a glass of Guinness won the war in Burma and the Western Desert, with only a minimum of manly sweat.

The post-war British studios flourished, many, like Ealing, prospering on their own house reputations. If anyone in film noticed television at all, it was to smile kindly and give it four out of ten for a poor imitation.

Early television drama suffered badly from claustrophobia. Chartres Cathedral was represented by three flats in a corner of a minute studio, one of which, if you were lucky, might have had a stained-glass window in it. Outdoor serials like *Treasure Island* and

Huckleberry Finn were done 'live' from the smallest BBC television studio at Lime Grove, with practically no film content at all. The woodland glades of Sherwood Forest were a handful of trees against a back-projection plate of Wimbledon Common. I remember one transmission where they had actually put in the background slide upside down. Patrick Troughton, playing Robin Hood, later told me that for one mad moment he had considered standing on his head, but realised that this would tax Friar Tuck unduly.

Filmed content was something of a luxury, and the cuts from film to studio were often so crude that even the viewers noticed. Children's television drama did much to pave the way for a regular injection of film into drama. Its scripts were adventures, packed with fights and chases and outdoor movement. This sort of action drama had to be produced from a studio little bigger than a millionaire's sitting room, and, as ambitions increased, film became a 'must', if the serials were to have any credibility.

By the sixties, film was an accepted ingredient of all drama; its fees and budgets were derisory compared with feature film, but television audiences were already in the millions, and the chance to communicate on such giant terms was attracting the best writing and directing talents; the use of film was a strong part of the attraction.

The newly-minted series drama, drawn from the American all-film pattern, was hungry for film, and the single play was not slow to claim its precedence. All-film plays led the way. They became a regular ingredient of *The Wednesday Play*, television's most remembered strand which set a pattern still fresh with *Play for Today*. It was created by such producers as James MacTaggart, Peter Luke, Irene Shubik, Graeme McDonald, Kenith Trodd; such directors as Kenneth Loach, Charles Jarrott, Christopher Morahan, Gareth Davies, Waris Hussein, Robin Midgeley, and a dozen more. The list of plays in this extraordinary strand is too rich to allow more than a dip in at random. There was Nell Dunn's *Up the Junction*, Jeremy Sandford's *Cathy Come Home*, Jim Allen's *The Lump*, David Mercer's *In Two Minds*, *Let's Murder Vivaldi*, and *On The Eve of Publication*, Neville Smith's *The Golden Vision*; Peter Nichol's *The Gorge*, Jim Allen's *The Big Flame*. Later, in the seventies, Tom Clarke's *Mad Jack* and *Stocker's Copper*, Jeremy Sandford's *Edna the Inebriate Woman*, Colin Welland's *Kisses at Fifty* and *Leeds United*, Mike Leigh's *Hard Labour*, Les Blair's *Blooming Youth*, John McGrath's *The Cheviot, the Stag and the Black Black Oil*,

Peter McDougall's *Just Another Saturday* and *Just a Boy's Game*, David Hare's *Licking Hitler*, Jim Allen's four-part *Days of Hope*, Jack Rosenthal's *The Evacuees*, Jim Allen's *The Spongers*, Dennis Potter's *Blue Remembered Hills*, G. F. Newman's *Law and Order*. All hard-edged plays that challenged, pushed out boundaries, upset people and got questions asked; and, in doing so, established the place of serious television drama.

The all film series followed later, with such titles as *The Sweeney*, *Target*, *Shoestring*, such quality serials as *Tinker, Tailor, Soldier, Spy*.

Every director wants to film, to get away from the theatrical confinement of the studio into the real world of concrete and horizons, the ugliness of industrial towns and suburbs; even, if pressed, the beauty of moorlands. There is a unique satisfaction in escaping with a compact, creative unit, shedding bureaucracy and paperwork and administrative frownings; to build up a film shot by shot, scene by scene, replacing words with images, taking and retaking performances until they are perfect. To know at the end of the day that you have actually completed one part of the whole – which is perfect, but may still be improved by editing and dubbing. Film is flexible up to its last moment of completion; it can be added to, subtracted from. Its physical manipulation is a pleasure.

It has become a convention to record the filmed part of a television drama first, moving into the studio for the rest, which is usually the greater part. That is how Hollywood did it. But there is no longer much logic to it. One can as sensibly post-film as pre-film, and in my opinion there are strong arguments for the former. Actors sent out on location to pre-record a few scenes for a thirteen-part series may commit themselves to performances they afterwards regret, when their errors are petrified on film. A few weeks of rehearsal, a couple of episodes recorded allows everyone – actor, director and writer – to have found out what the drama is really about. To argue that many of television's most successful series were made in this fashion is no real answer; much that was done in those early days was done perforce.

Filming is expensive, by far the most costly unit in television drama. Partly because of this cost, and partly because they have built themselves rows of electronic studios, the great television organisations have accepted the compromise of part-film part-studio for the major part of its fictional output. What the future holds is anyone's guess. The high walls between film and tape are being methodically tumbled down; tape has evicted film from its monopoly of the location scene in TV drama. To use studios for one mode only, or even more absurd, simply because they exist, is financial sense but artistic nonsense. Perhaps we shall reach a time when studios can be used for either mode, tape or film; a suggestion so logical that every entertainment union in the land must challenge it.

Admitting, for the moment, that the director will follow these old conventions of pre-filming, the next stage is to break down the script into its components. Some sequences are obviously film – car chases, burning buildings, volcanic eruptions, docksides – backgrounds impossible to reproduce credibly in the studio. There may be less obvious claimants; scenes involving stunts or tricks, illusions, difficult fights, which will surely be more effective filmed, in that they are controllable. Once, in a 'live' transmission I had an actor literally knocked out in a fight; the battle raged on over his prone body and it was only by the grace of God that he came round in time for his next line, which was supposed to be a triumphant and ringing announcement of his victory, but emerged as a quavering whisper from the edge of the grave. Additional filming may be those scenes which would otherwise have to be shot against back projection in the studio – the interior of moving cars, hilltops, riversides . . .

Even the simplest filming involves a platoon of experts. Behind the camera there must be, irreplaceably, a lighting cameraman and his crew, designers and scenemen to create and adjust the backgrounds, property men to dress them. Costume and make-up must be there to serve the actors, drivers to bring them to the locations and back again. The director will have his own essential assistants, to keep the unit moving and happy, and financially afloat; to produce impossibilities demanded by the director at the drop of a shot-list. There are specialists like the armourer, who is there to look after any guns used by the unit, and make sure they will not go off at any time, except the all-important 'take'. There may be visual effects, to blow the location up. There will be actors waiting impatiently for their scenes, and a bus load of extras in Chinese armour. There may even be an anxious writer, determined to defend his script, his every last line to the death.

Whoever they are, they will be hungry every few hours. This means there must be a nearby café or restaurant, willing to serve sixty hot lunches three hours late; or, more satisfactory, a location catering firm, run by professionals who specialise in feeding large units at any hour of the night and day. Any good caterer will conjure up cups of coffee at two o'clock in the morning; and a good production assistant will make sure that there is something stronger in them than coffee.

If the filming is of any duration, the whole unit must be put up at convenient hotels; if they are abroad, there will be air transport. There will be vehicles carrying equipment, properties and costumes which must be got to the location.

Nowhere in location work is there any guarantee that everything will go according to plan. One thing at least will go hideously wrong. When the BBC serial *War and Peace* was being planned it was decided to film extensively in Yugoslavia, not least because the Yugoslav Army still had some cavalry, which they promised to hire out. The famous retreat from Moscow was most carefully plotted. The Yugoslavs assured us that a certain district in northern Yugoslavia had had deep snow in the required month every year for the past two centuries.

The unit consequently presented itself, cavalry and all, at this wintry spot, to find green fields and warm sunshine. Useless for the Yugoslavs to protest that it had never happened before. How could one credibly conduct the retreat from Moscow without snow? The expensive answer was to uproot the entire unit and take it hundreds of miles further north, where a thin grudging layer of snow gave some appearance of Tolstoy's original scene.

Most directors have at some time arrived on location to find the factory/shop/water tower/public lavatory, of their choice, has been ruthlessly bulldozed to flat ground in the interval between his recce and the filming. I arrived on a remote country location in Sussex to film British prisoners of war escaping across country, pursued by platoons of German soldiers, vehicles crammed with SS, tanks and armoured cars. When I got to the location I found it swathed in a deep fog, choking and impenetrable; but not a real fog for the local farmers had decided to spray their wide fields with pest-killer, or oat encourager, or whatever it was, from an aeroplane. Filming was off for that day; how could one find the farmers, implore them to stop and get the message through to their busy aircraft? And who, even in the most efficient production team, could have guessed at such a bizarre possibility?

In any television drama time is money. In filming it is a small fortune. But efficient planning can reduce the bill from impossible to appalling. Movement is time-consuming and travelling time cuts into the hours of shooting, so the more the locations can be clustered the better.

Filming is hard work. Even the most efficient unit works under pressure. In England, there is an unequal battle against the inconstant weather. For financial reasons, television schedules seem to work on the happy assumption that the sun shines from five in the morning till ten at night. Yet a well-run unit, working steadily to put a few minutes of quality film in the can each day, can be a joy. Much of this depends on the director. If the unit likes and trusts him, it will relax and enjoy the location.

By contrast, a disorganised director can drive everyone mad. Everyone knows him. He is the one who has done no homework, who stands undecided as the light fades, wondering what to do next, how to do it, whether to do it all. He believes in working by flair – 'off the top of his head'. He is a great bore to actors, who resent being used as pawns in his inept game of chess. He overloads his schedule to the point of incredulity, calling for fifty scenes on the shortest day of the winter.

Time governs all. Time to set up, to light the scenes, to rehearse the action; time to move from set-up to set-up, to travel; spare time to absorb the natural disasters that attack all film units – vehicles breaking down, cameras seizing up, actors not arriving. Every schedule should have its built-in 'rain-cover' – plans to move to interior shooting if bad weather persists. It is not always practical – there may be no interior alternative – but there should always be something to which an ailing film schedule can turn.

Modern films stock can accept light levels which were impossible a few years ago. But a visual consistency must be maintained from shot to shot; there is a limit to what may be smoothed out by processing.

It goes without saying (yet, amazingly, it still happens) that a film crew must not arrive unannounced in a busy street, a private factory, or on a public beach, on the optimistic assumption that everyone will stop what they are doing and co-operate with your exciting, lovable film unit. The British public is long-suffering, but it only requires one irate citizen (who knows his rights) to bring the whole enterprise to a costly halt. Prior permission must be sought from the owners of land and property, from local authorities, above all from the police, to whom the increasing presence of television units has become a rising irritation. Nothing upsets a policeman more than unexpectedly coming across a film unit on his local high street realistically shooting a raid on the district bank. Long before such an event, the production must have sought and obtained permission to be there at all. If private property is to be used, be it a shed or a stately home, a facility fee may have to be agreed. Nowadays everyone has heard of this useful addition to income, and the most astonishing sums are demanded for small services. Any fee, however, is cheaper than building an entire set from scratch.

The printed schedule for a television film unit is like a route march order for a regiment, though probably more efficient. It will contain, obviously, the names and telephone numbers of all concerned, cast and staff. It will have maps, indicating the exact position of the locations, and the centres from which the unit will operate. In military terms, it will supply route orders, the times of trains and buses leaving base, the details of each day's anticipated shooting, the rest days, and what to do if you get lost. It will set out precise instructions as to the movement of scenery, properties, equipment, costumes and make-up, with hopeful times of loading and delivery. It allocates parking spaces, and will note that electricians will bring generators with them, which must be parked far enough from the location so as not to be heard. A good film schedule is a sort of Bible, without the morality.

Foreign filming adds the complication of flights, minute details of local back-up, interpreters and bizarre foreign customs. But in the end it is no different from any other filming, apart from the fact that no one on the unit speaks Turkish.

If the filming is extensive, with long dialogue scenes, there must be adequate rehearsals before the unit move off or on the location site. If the whole script is on film, complete rehearsals are essential if a final shooting script and the actors' performances are to be stabilised.

Scripts may well have been sent to the actor in advance, from which he will have gauged the size of his part, and the general line of the plot. But only rehearsal with the rest of the cast will properly determine what the play is about. This sort of pre-rehearsal, once a luxury, has proved itself essential. Hollywood was content to build up its films scene by scene with a minimum of rehearsal before each take. They had infinite time to retake if things went awry. Scenarios were fragmented, shot piecemeal and out of sequence, and the actors must have leaned heavily on the directors to keep their performances on course. Apocryphal stories abound, amongst which I particularly like the one about Robert Mitchum, an effective film star noted for the almost total lack of expression on his face, whatever the dramatic situation confronting him. On one occasion Mitchum was about to record a simple reaction close-up. The young director, a disciple of the method school, went into a passionate explanation about the psychology of the shot, and the emotions that must surge through Mitchum's brain during it. He reminded the astonished actor that his mother (in the script) had turned to prostitution, whilst his father (still in the script) had been a drunken wreck serving a life sentence in Alcatraz. He spoke volubly of childhood traumas, of the deep unhappiness of adolescence, of rejection. Mitchum listened sleepily, but finally raised a commanding hand. 'Listen, son,' he said. 'I can look right of camera, I can look left of camera. Which you gonna have?'

A wholly satisfying statement. But one still wonders how the excellent pace and balance of so many Hollywood films was achieved.

Location filming is never short of reasons to go wrong. Even the best of directors fall behind schedule, for the best of reasons. The weather is always out of sympathy with the script; if wet weather is essential, it will be the record drought of all time. There will be breakdowns and mysterious stoppages, sometimes caused by unions who appear to be only remotely connected with entertainment.

There may be illness amongst the cast, though this is rare, for actors cannot afford to be ill. There may even be an acute case of miscasting, though this is mercifully infrequent. Or it may be simply the usual irrational, lunatic bad luck.

I once found myself at two o'clock in the morning on a lonely Suffolk beach, which we were pretending was the coast of France in the Second World War. The scene was simple enough. Three British agents, led by the gallant Captain Francis Matthews, paddle an inflatable dinghy out of the darkness of the sea to the shore, spring lightly on to the beach, and drag the dinghy up it; one of them then plunges a knife into it, deflating it, and making it possible to bury it in the shingle. All the ingredients of adventure were there. The cliff was lined with large lamps ('It will be a full moon tonight, Henri') and actors playing the French Resistance sipped coffee as our three heroes prepared to board their frail craft.

It was here that a major error was discovered. The inflatable dinghy had a sizeable leak, and there was only a small bicycle pump to keep this under control. This posed a problem. How could three agents land from the sea if they had nothing to land from? Could they possibly have swum the whole way from England? Absurd.

A feature film company would have 'wrapped' for the night and returned next day. We hadn't got a next day. The problem was solved by the simple expedient of loading the dinghy on to a van, driving it two miles to a dark garage, knocking up the angry owner, bribing him and borrowing his air supply to fill the dinghy to bursting point. Then back to the beach, pumping furiously with the bicycle pump all the way. Down over the cliffs and into the sea, still pumping. Our three heroes were thrust unceremoniously into the dinghy and pushed out into the darkness of the North Sea. The camera turned; our three agents paddled ashore with a desperation not acted. They reached the shore in a sort of soggy bag, dragged it up the beach and quite unnecessarily plunged a knife into what was by then no more than a limp rag.

To their credit the actors completed the scene with suitable tension, but there was general hysteria afterwards. The unit felt that, on the whole, it had once more achieved the impossible.

A trivial incident that underlines the great gap between feature film making, and its television equivalent. Films today cost millions, and they cost millions because they spend money absurdly. Television does not have that sort of money, and has been forced into more sensible ways. The TV results, at best, are not always so different from much that is fed into the cinemas.

Filming requires patience. The process cannot be rushed. Each scene must be rehearsed for the actors and for the camera. It must be lit and relit, for every angle of the scene, and a good lighting cameraman will not compromise, any more than the leading actors will.

Film is an exact science, served by experts, who will not readily compromise. They will expect each scene to be technically and artistically as good as possible. For the director, as for the actor, this means a lot of irritated pacing about whilst others get on with their work.

The director can best speed up the general rate of work by knowing precisely what he wants; by being definite about the current scene, and even more decisive about the next to be shot. Intelligent anticipation saves a lot of aggravation on location. Units like a director who knows his mind. They cordially detest the one who suddenly discovers, when the entire unit has moved ten miles to the next location, that he has left out three vital scenes from the last location.

The acceptance by the British public of the unusual and the outré

1 *The Final Test* (1951): an original play for television by Terence Rattigan

2 *The Pickwick Papers* (1952): an early Dickens serial nerve-rackingly produced 'live' in the tiny Alexandra Palace studio. With George Howe as Mr Pickwick

3 George Orwell's *1984* (1954): one of television drama's early major events. With Peter Cushing and André Morell

4 *The Grove Family* (1957): the first television soap opera, so named after the Lime Grove Studios in which it was produced; with Sam Jephcott, Margaret Downs, Ruth Dunning, Christopher Beeny and Edward Evans

5 A scene from the great Shakespearean television event *An Age of Kings* (1960) with Frank Pettingell as Falstaff and Robert Hardy as Prince Hal in *Henry IV Part 1*

6 Sean Connery as Vronsky in Rudolph Cartier's *Anna Karenina* (1961)

7 An early production of *Wuthering Heights* (1962) with Keith Michell and Claire Bloom: an example of how the wild Yorkshire moors can be realistically reproduced in a small studio

8 *Z Cars* (1962), the police series that overnight introduced a new pattern of terse writing, fast cutting and close camera shooting; it also did a great deal to change the public image of the policeman. Shaun Sutton was one of its first directors

9 *The Largest Theatre in the World* was an attempt to establish a series of major plays to which most of the countries of Europe would contribute. The 1962 play was Terence Rattigan's *Heart to Heart* with Ralph Richardson and Kenneth More

10 *Detective* was a series of plays adapted from crime novels. *The Moving Toy Shop* (1964) by Edmund Crispin, adapted by John Hopkins and directed by Shaun Sutton, was the opening production. With Richard Wordsworth, Nicholas Pennell and John Wood

11 The very first *Wednesday Play*, *Alice* (1965) by Dennis Potter, soon to become television's most provocative playwright. With Deborah Watling, John Saunders, Peter Barlett and John Bailey

12 One of the most memorable of *Wednesday Plays*, Nell Dunn's *Up the Junction* (1965), with Vickery Turner and Tony Selby

13 The most famous play in television history: Jeremy Sandford's *Cathy Come Home* (1966) which led directly to the charity Shelter. Carol White as Cathy and Ray Brooks as Reg

14 Maurice Denham and Judi Dench in *Talking to a Stranger* (1966), a quartet of plays which presented the same event from the point of view of each of the four characters

16 *The Six Wives of Henry VIII* (1970): one of the most successful of the play series in colour. With Keith Michell as Henry

15 *Opposite: The Forsyte Saga* (1966): one of the most famous families in television whose story became a viewing event all over the world

17 *The Roads to Freedom* (1970) was a thirteen-part dramatisation of the three war-time novels of Jean-Paul Sartre. Michael Bryant as Mathieu

18 *Left: Elizabeth R* (1971): the natural follow-up to Henry VIII, starring Glenda Jackson as Elizabeth. In such series colour showed the period costumes to their best dramatic effect

19 *Opposite:* Patricia Hayes as *Edna the Inebriate Woman* (1971), Jeremy Sandford's second great play for television

21 *Above:* An all-film *Play for Today* of Tom Clarke's *Stocker's Copper* (1972), shot entirely on location in Cornwall. With Bryan Marshall and Jane Lapotaire

20 *Opposite: Upstairs, Downstairs:* a 1970s' television success on both sides of the Atlantic. With Gordon Jackson, David Langton and Jean Marsh

22 *Below:* A scene from *The Brothers* (1972), one of the most popular of the long-running series of the 1970s. With Robin Chadwick, Glyn Owen, Jean Anderson and Richard Easton

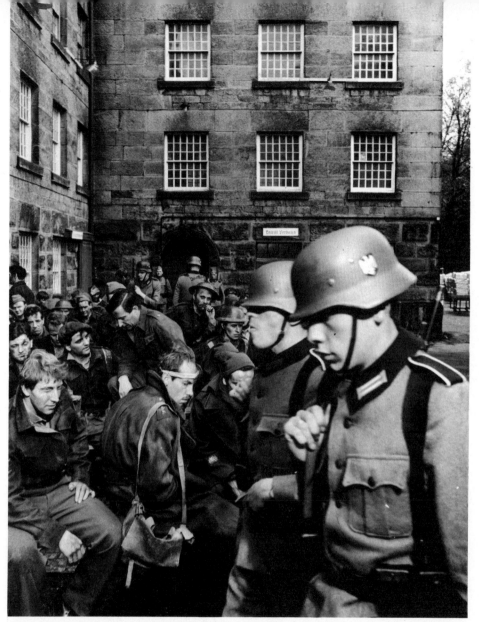

24 *Colditz* (1972): one of the best known prison camp series

23 *Opposite:* The retreat from Moscow (set in Yugoslavia and featuring the Yugoslav Army) as seen in the twenty-episode version of Tolstoy's *War and Peace* (1972)

25 *Left:* One of the great stars of television, the late Jack Warner, as Sergeant George Dixon in *Dixon of Dock Green*, a police series that spanned twenty-one years, from 1955 to 1976

27 *Opposite: Shoulder to Shoulder* (1974): six plays dramatising the long hard fight by the Suffragettes to win the vote for women. Lined up for battle are Sian Phillips, Patricia Quinn, Angela Down, Georgia Brown and Judy Parfitt

26 *Quatermass and the Pit* (1973): the third of the hugely popular Quatermass science fiction serials. With Andrew Keir as Professor Quatermass and James Donald as Dr Ronay

28 *Left: The Pallisers* (1974): a not entirely successful attempt to adapt the six Trollope novels into twenty-four episodes, retrieved by performances by, amongst others, Philip Latham and Susan Hampshire

30 *Opposite:* Michael Horden in a Jonathan Miller production of *King Lear* (1975), a partnership they reformed in 1982 for a new production of the play produced by Shaun Sutton for the BBC Shakespeare series

29 Jack Rosenthal's prize-winning *The Evacuees* (1975): an all-film play about young evacuees during the Second World War

31 Tony Garnett's production *Days of Hope* (1975): four filmed plays covering the fortunes of three young people from 1916 to the General Strike. A conscientious objector being forced over the trench parapet into No Man's Land

32 *The Naked Civil Servant* (1975) starring John Hurt: one of the many plays reflecting the more liberal climate in drama during the 1970s.

33 Tom Conti and Prunella Gee in Frederick Raphael's successful television series *The Glittering Prizes* (1976)

34 *Above: I, Claudius* (1976), the late Jack Pulman's all-studio adaptation of the two Robert Graves novels. Excellent design, costume and make-up contributed towards making this an immaculate production. With Sian Phillips and Brian Blessed

36 *Opposite:* Ian Holm as J M Barrie in the drama trilogy *The Lost Boys* (1978)

35 *Below: Philby, Burgess and Maclean*, an excellent example of drama taken from real life. With Michael Culver as Maclean and Derek Jacobi as Burgess

37 *Pennies from Heaven* (1978): a play series of startling originality by Dennis Potter, combining the popular songs of the 1930s with a story of moral decline and murder. With Bob Hoskins and Cheryl Campbell

38 A scene from one of television's most joyful series *All Creatures Great and Small* (1979) which attracted enormous audiences throughout the country. With Robert Hardy and Christopher Timothy

39 Alec Guinness and Sian Phillips in the all-film adaptation of John Le Carré's *Tinker, Tailor, Soldier, Spy* (1979)

40 *Opposite:* The longest-running science fiction of all time: Tom Baker as the fourth in line Dr Who with Lalla Ward in the series that has charmed children and adults for nineteen years

41 *Right:* School serials have always had a place in television drama. John Duttine and Frank Middlemas in one of the latest of them: *To Serve Them All My Days* (1980)

42 Philip Madoc as Lloyd George in one of the later episodes of the serial *The Life and Times of David Lloyd George* (1981), produced entirely by the Welsh section of BBC Drama

43 *Brideshead Revisited*: the lavish adaptation of Evelyn Waugh's novel that became a television event. With Anthony Andrew as Sebastian Flyte and Jeremy Irons as Charles Ryder

44 *Opposite:* Judi Dench with the thalidomide boy, Terry Wiles, whose story was so movingly told in *On Giant's Shoulders* (1982), a play that won top awards in England and America

45 *Above:* A small BBC film unit shooting a scene for *David Copperfield* in 1956. Since then television film units have grown enormously in the number of people involved and in the proliferation of their equipment

47 *Opposite:* Shaun Sutton (fourth from right) directing an early live episode of *Z Cars* from the gallery

46 *Below:* Filming the death of Lee Harvey Oswald in the drama documentary about the assassination of President Kennedy: *Lee Oswald – Assassin* (1966)

48 & 49 The make-up artist 'ageing' Glenda Jackson for *Elizabeth R* (1971) and Sian
Phillips for *I, Claudius* (1976)

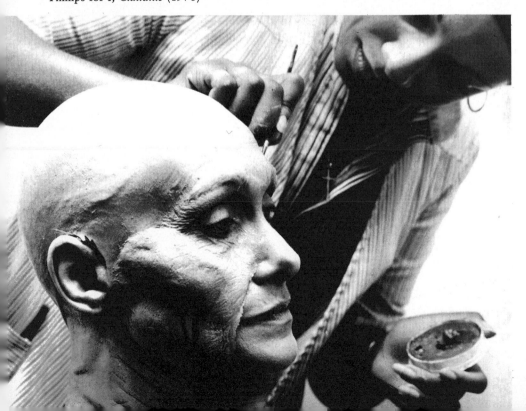

is traditional. A drunk man can strip himself naked in Trafalgar Square and play the zither standing on his head, and the public, more embarrassed *for* him than by him, will pass with averted eyes. So it is with filming. I have had an actor in full armour standing in a bus queue, and no one raised an eyebrow. The only difficulty arose when he had boarded the bus and found he had no pocket from which to take his fare. I had the same actor in a crowded street with a tray of real one pound notes, trying to give them away. The public, deeply embarrassed by this eccentricity, passed by on the other side.

Less than twenty years ago, the public attitude to filming was less blasé; nowadays it seems that every corner has its television unit. If I ever tried to rob a bank I would put up a camera and a few lights outside, and then take the bank for every penny it had. No one would stop me. It would be just some more of that television filming.

When newcomers ask me if filming is difficult, I always feel like saying that it depends on how difficult the filming is. A riot in Piccadilly Circus during the rush hour, with a tanker overturning, is *very* difficult; a car driving out of a factory in Park Royal is easy. Twenty Cavaliers fighting fifty Roundheads in a Bath backstreet poses problems. A secret agent crossing Lake Como in a motor launch is not only simple to film but pleasant. There are difficult set-ups and easy ones. A motor cycle with Kate Nelligan on the pillion pulling up outside a Kenton semi-detached may sagely be left to the production assistant who is dying to prove he can do it – especially with Kate Nelligan.

Film 'rushes', the rough prints of the previous day's shooting, are part of the rhythm of filming. It is essential to know that the results are technically successful, even if there are no doubts about the performances. A location close to base – say, a BBC unit working close to Ealing Studios – will present no problems. The director himself can probably slip over and view the 'rushes'. The important thing is that information should be available as soon as possible, so that if anything has failed, it can be reshot before the unit moved on to other sequences. If the location is Wigan or Wilhelmshaven, there is no question of anyone from the unit seeing the rushes next day. They must be viewed by the producer, an assistant, by *someone* whom the director trusts and can rely on to report on them professionally.

Rushes, or the best of them, can be transferred to cassette and sent post haste to the location; this is often done. For no matter how glowing the reports, directors fret until they have actually seen their work, as do lighting cameramen, make-up artists and others on the unit. Oddly enough, many actors hate rushes, and prefer not to see them.

Getting the right pace on a film script is an art in itself. A stage play rehearses in one piece; it may be run and run again until its mistakes and longueurs, overwritings and omissions are evident to the most insensitive director; and any faults not ironed out in rehearsal become doubly evident when the play is given its public preview performances. Pace is not just going fast. It is a variation of tempo, and it may be the making of a play, emphasising its moments of truth, adding colour by contrast. Those dramas mainly recorded in the studio will have been fully rehearsed as one piece, and their pacing preregulated. But a film – any film – is shot in small fragments, and rarely in the natural sequence of its scenes. There are always unarguable reasons why the end must be done first, the beginning last, and the middle spread over three widely separated sessions; reasons of economy, convenience, availability of artists or locations. Weeks may separate a highly emotional scene from the one immediately preceding it, and the one to follow. Actors need a special filmic skill to bridge these gaps, if they are to retain any constancy in their performances. The director must hold not only these performances in his mind, but the rhythm of the production in all its aspects.

A variety of pace can undoubtedly be achieved by skilful editing, for editing and pace are indivisible. But only the director can know the whole script *absolutely*. He must be so steeped in it that he can drop into it at any point, and know precisely how that scene is to be acted, shot, stressed and paced.

It is a great deal easier to say than to do; and it is not a skill that can be taught; it must be there in the director from the beginning.

Independent production in television is the order of the day. Small companies either operate with the big organisations, using their hardware and services or work entirely on their own. *Telford's Change* was an example of the first – a ten-part serial brought complete to the BBC Drama Group by producer Mark Shivas, writer Brian Clark and actor Peter Barkworth. The serial was serviced and recorded at the BBC, financial contract having been struck between the two parties. It is a form of production that is undoubtedly on the increase, and will play a robust part in the making of programmes for ITV2 (Channel Four).

Other companies are literally independent, making their programmes totally free of the established organisations and using one of the many 'supply' houses to service their editing and post-production. But television drama is expensive, and the all-film play or serial are very expensive. Many of the true independents will operate widely on location, using either film or tape. Neither operation is cheap.

There is nothing new about making programmes all on tape on location. Sport, current affairs, events and news have been at it for years. Coronations and state funerals are transmitted as they happen, live, and tape-recorded *en route*.

What was new, some dozen years ago, was the suggestion that drama might be made this way at an infinitely higher rate of productivity, and thus, at a lower cost. Every television accountant (and how their numbers have grown) knows that time spent on location is a fortune spent. The cost of keeping even the most modest unit on the road rises yearly with the rate of inflation, and any scheme that could produce the same results as film at less cost was worth considering. Early tape-on-location dramas achieved, on occasion, a quite astonishing productivity – ten, twelve, even more minutes a day. The 1979 figure was something over six minutes a day average, as opposed to two and a half minutes on film.

Yet film can also do it. The director Roland Joffe, filming Ford's *'Tis Pity She's a Whore*, in and around a stately home, achieved the two and a quarter hours of a very difficult play in twenty-one days – six and a half minutes per day – an astonishing feat made possible by his own efficiency, and his capacity to inspire every member of his unit.

On average, however, tape has the edge on productivity; if the general film rate could be increased to five and a half minutes per day, there would be little to choose between the cost of the two operations. Filming is traditionally, often mysteriously, slow. Tony Garnett, who has done more than anyone in television to establish the all-film drama, turned up an interesting statistic in a report he made on Fiction Programmes some years ago. He said: 'If three minutes of cut film a day is achieved, and the shooting ratio is ten to one, then the camera was turning for just *thirty minutes*. What happened to the rest of the day? Was it all taken up with the necessary preliminaries?'

If productivity is a powerful argument, there are others. Film has to be processed and, until you have seen the rushes, there can be no absolute certainty that the scenes you think to be perfect have turned out as you hoped. The performances may have been excellent – but the stock may have been ruined by the laboratories, or in your own camera. It happens. There may have been a 'hair in the gate', one of those irritating squiggles that squirm about in the picture; there may be 'sparkle' on the print, a sort of constellation of flashing dots; or thick black lines scored down the centre of your film.

With tape you can see at once what you have shot; you just rerun the tape. You can check performances, lighting, framing. It also enables you to check points of continuity between scenes, or between shots: the position of an actor's hand, of a chair, the direction in which a character was looking, even such trivia as the length of ash on a cigar, or the level of drink in a glass.

Tape will accept degrees of light that film may reject; you can continue to shoot longer as the light goes. Moreover, if you are shooting a scene of any length on, say, two cameras (and several minutes is 'of length') a sudden change of light, the sun going behind a cloud, will not be so disastrous as a radical light change between a sequence of shots in a filmed scene. If the drama is to be mainly studio recorded and inserts are being shot, the matching between location and studio can be that much more natural – for it is tape to tape.

Lastly, and I suppose obviously, tape dispenses not only with the delays of film processing, but their cost. Though the cynics will be quick to insist that other charges are substituted.

The critics of tape-on-location have never been short of ammunition. They point to the remarkable fluidity of the film camera, with its built-in recording mechanism; no cumbersome cables spun out across hundreds of feet of countryside to the recording vehicle; an argument that will no doubt soon be defunct, for cable may soon be dispensed with altogether in the tape operation.

A more potent objection is the physical stance of the director himself. In film, he stands by the camera, in close contact with cast and cameraman. With tape he must move between the scene and the recording vehicle – the scanner – with its monitors, its cutting and recording facilities. The two may be a quarter of a mile apart.

Film buffs will argue that the lightweight film camera, with its single eye on the scene, is a purer, more technically perfect, tool for production; each scene is separately set up, rehearsed, and lit. In tape (as in the studio) the lighting must often serve for a variety of angles of the scene. But even this applies less as more and more tape-on-location directors work with one camera only.

Tape critics put their money on the flexibility of film editing and post-production, sound and picture. But tape editing, and dubbing, have reached an extremely sophisticated level. It can be claimed that it now lacks little that film editing can supply.

Tony Garnett again: 'Tape and electronics will win out eventually. New technology always does. Film is a product of nineteenth-century technology – sprocket holes, a chain mechanism, a few chemicals put in layers on the stock ... tape equipment will continue to get lighter and more flexible, and will overtake film ... it will all merge in some form, taking the best and cheapest qualities from both. But it will all be part of the transformation in exhibition, which will affect the cinema *and* broadcasting. ...'

Later, in the same letter, he added: 'At the moment I prefer film. But I'm keeping an eye on developments. It's an exciting life, and it'll get even more exciting in the eighties. ...'

John Glenister, a director equally at home on tape or film, added his own wry comparison: 'Film making is washing by hand, as against the launderette of the video process.' Michael Darlow, who directed *Crime and Punishment* and *Suez*, summed up the feelings of many directors about the flexibility of film shooting and editing, and their relation to each other: 'For me, above all, films are made in the cutting room, by the slow and intensely satisfying collage-like process which gives such flexibility and control.' I would only add that he must first have the great acting performances to control.

There is a great deal of controversy about picture quality. Rodney Bennett, who directed *The Lost Boys* and *Hamlet*, said: 'The picture quality of exteriors shot on OB cameras is sometimes not as aesthetically pleasing as that shot on film ... the picture quality on film can be further controlled and adjusted in the processing stage.'

It is certainly true that tape pictures can be *too* good, unnaturally sharp and precise, with a depth of focus stretching to the horizon. Such perfection can have a false look. Film addicts underline the special strengths of the successful film unit out on location – a community close-knit, on a communal creative course, living and eating together, building as they go.

Michael Darlow again: 'Ultimately, one is trying to create teams of people who stimulate each other, who are involved in, and proud of, what they are doing. ...'

I suspect that this point of view may fast go out of date. With the increasing sophistications of OB (outside broadcast) drama (that is drama shot entirely on tape on location), the fact that complete plays and serials are now made on tape on location, this close-knit community spirit exists in both, and both produce the same end-product – a complete drama.

Tony Garnett: 'The fact that film on the one hand, and OB on the other use different methods should not blind us to the similarities of technique and working in the making of location fiction ... the similarities of technique and working practices on location are likely to increase.'

Looking into the future, Tony expressed what many of us recognise and hope to see: a total cross-fertilisation of film and OB crews at every level – OB staff with film sound recordists, tape and film cameramen, film and video lighting. In the end, surely, we must have crews who will tackle any sort of recording process.

Writers have always written specially for the different media – film, theatre, television studio or TV film. They must now write specially for this newest form. It is not enough for a producer to glance at a script and say 'A lot of this seems to take place in a garden – just right for an OB'. The OB could substitute for the filming of the garden scenes, but it is the whole script that must fit. In a perfect world the writer would know in advance what OB drama time was available, and be asked to come up with ideas for it; ideally, he could visit the location before writing the scenes.

Many of the qualities that cry out for film can obviously be satisfied by OB – the need to get away from studio restrictions, for wide canvases, rivers and hillsides and the texture of real walls. Where film still has an edge is with scripts full of widespread action, car chases, movements over difficult terrain, scenes in awkward corners or on the top of mountains. Here compactness and lightness are the rules of the game.

Where OB has the edge is with scripts that have long dialogue and group scenes; when the action is confined to a reasonably controllable area and the use of two cameras together can be an asset. I doubt if most of the arguments either way will be relevant for long, for tape-on-location has moved a long way since its first unsteady steps, and the two modes are moving even closer together. But that the writer should know for what mode he is writing remains as important in tape as in other methods of recording.

Drama tape-on-location was born of the personal convictions of a handful of people in drama, aided and abetted by like enthusiasts in the electronic and engineering corners of drama. Television consumes scripts and ideas hungrily, and, however hard you try to be individual, a lot of it comes out looking much the same. The chance of an entirely fresh look was a challenge. Film had already added one new dimension to studio plays; tape could add another.

The early experiments had to be made with the only equipment available – the weighty four-camera units used normally for sports and coronations. The cameras were huge and heavy, the cabling like elephants' trunks, and there was a whole wagon train of supplementary vehicles that had to be parked and hidden away. Trailing this cavalcade round the countryside might have depressed the most lunatic enthusiasts (who included David Attenborough and me) but persistence paid off. The BBC recorded *A Midsummer Night's Dream, The Little Minister, The Recruiting Officer, The London Assurance* and Solzhenitsyn's *The Love Girl and the Innocent*, shot in an abandoned RAF camp in North Norfolk, which looked (and felt) astonishingly like Siberia.

Why we chose such long and difficult plays for our baptism remains something of a mystery. Actually, the very first to be recorded in the new way was a splendid little thirty-minute play called *A Question of Honour* – a true and quite incredible story of how an English soldier was shot for killing a German soldier at the beginning of the First World War; apparently he broke the rules and did it the wrong way. Or something.

The crew, entirely new to fictional scripts, were determined to show that they could make it work. They had every sort of problem – immobility, awkward sound (shooting in a small, panelled Elizabethan room gave everyone hollow 'boxy' voices, and footsteps sounded like an army in flight). The lighting engineers were tackling a new version of their craft; overnight, they were coping with multiple angles and set-ups, low-key night scenes, shadow problems, light cues, graded light to suggest sunset, lamplight, candles . . . They had to produce it without the blessing and flexibility of studio equipment, where light can be produced from any angle, any height, direct or by reflection. The cameramen, so quick and adept at sports and events, had to learn the subtleties of drama framing and grouping. That these early productions arrived at all is a tribute to enthusiasm.

The new mode produced surprising mistakes. Experienced directors who, in film or studio, would have shot tight on their actors and groups, became strangely obsessed with long views of geography and architecture. The early tape-on-location productions are rich in rolling moorland, sweeping panoramas, with the actors inch high, trying to get in an audible word against the roar of a nearby waterfall.

A similar madness prevailed in the interiors. Throughout the stately homes of England, actresses descended magnificent Adam staircases, or paced endless corridors, wordless and silent till they finally reached the camera; by which time the scene had died of ennui.

Seemingly, the hard-won conventions of television shooting, the close look and the intimacy of the small screen, were forgotten; all the more curious because, given a film camera, those same directors would have shot the plays quite differently. Perhaps it had something to do with the sulky inflexibility of the equipment.

It wasn't long before that was put right. Lighter units arrived, smaller cameras that could be hand-held, compact recording facilities, smaller vehicles and fewer of them, lighter and longer cables. Today's equipment is fast approaching a parity with film.

Future predictions in television are dangerous. In this particular tape/film controversy, productivity probably remains the key; and here tape is tending to erode one of its prime advantages. What started as a four-camera operation, and became a lightweight two-camera unit, is now threatening to become a single-camera operation, with the second camera used sparingly, often only to 'leapfrog' to the next set-up; which is admittedly a time-saving device in itself. But using only the single camera has automatically produced a sharp increase in editing and post-production; and this alone must tend to bring the cost of the two operations yet closer together.

Both systems are there for the asking; there is a measure of choice, on a horses-for-courses basis – the system fitting the script or the inclination of the director. But in the stringent years ahead, cost will be paramount. As the artistic and technical advantages of the two forms become identical, money may have the final say.

9

The Director:
Rehearsal and Studio

Like any new work for theatre or cinema, a television drama will transform itself on its journey to completion; the end product may be radically different from the first draft. Diligent rehearsal finds weaknesses in the best script, a matter not for dismay but celebration, for drama is the product of a variety of talents. A bad director can ruin a fine script, and poor casting can complete the destruction. On the happier side, a good director with an excellent cast can rescue a script that is struggling to be even mediocre.

Until recently, the testing ground for the West End play was the pre-London tour. There were dozens of 'number one dates', major provincial theatres, and the long-suffering citizens of Leeds and Brighton were guinea pigs to show the writer, director and actor what was wrong with their creation. They were seasoned audiences who had paid for the pleasure, and they were quick to register delight or disappointment. Comedies in particular benefited, establishing what the audience would laugh at and, more discouraging, what they would not. These tours were used as a time for experiment and rewriting, and the patient casts were recalled day after day to rehearse new scenes and reshape the old ones. No one minded – getting the play right for a long West End run was worth any trouble.

Today, although national tours are shorter, London plays do not open 'cold'; the managements run a series of preview performances, open to anyone but the critics; a measure of commonsense insurance in a very expensive operation.

Television is an instant performance medium; it cannot try out its dramas in front of the public. However thoroughly rehearsed, the play arrives at its recording day 'cold' in the theatrical sense, without the excitement and adrenalin of an opening night. Even the dullest theatrical opening is a time of tension and temperament, and it is not surprising that the first night has produced some of the theatre's unkindest jokes.

For example, the actress who goes round to the dressing room of her greatest rival after the first performance and says, 'Darling, I don't care what *anyone* says, I thought you were good,' leaving the unfortunate actress with the conviction that the whole theatre was ringing with her failure.

After days of hectic recording, a director will be warm in his thanks and lavish in his hospitality. But the aftermath is frequently an anticlimax, without public applause and congratulation. However well it has gone, no one can be certain that the segments will cut together into success. The drama, so painfully built up over weeks of rehearsal, has been ruthlessly fragmented by the process of recording; for which reason alone, a TV drama and its performances must be solidly fixed by the time of its translation from rehearsal room to studio.

Up to this moment, the drama has been rehearsed as one continuing whole, in the scriptual sense, broken up though it is into short scenes and shots, and punctuated by filmed inserts. In this way, it has been no different from any dramatic rehearsal – satisfying, dismaying, frustrating, exciting, depressing and inspiring by turns; the testing time for the director, and the most exciting for the one fortunate enough to have a good script and a cast to match it.

There is a moment in rehearsal when what has been up to then no more than a steady building of performances clicks into something exhilarating; when the script comes alive, the actors sparkle and bounce off each other. Suddenly it is better than you ever have hoped. It may never happen at all. The script may be mediocre, and the cast not skilful enough to disguise the fact. The director himself may not be good enough.

The location work is done. The rest of the script, probably the bulk of it, has now to be rehearsed. It may be a single play, the first of a trilogy or the opening episode of a series of six, ten or thirteen.

The ancient relationship between actor and director is as strong in television as in any other medium. *Hamlet* for television is the same play as *Hamlet* for the National Theatre, or the Olivier film, the difference lying only in its interpretation and the way it is presented.

Theatre everywhere is in financial straits. Plays are either locked into single settings; if there have to be several sets, they are often *suggested* by stylised scenery – an idea that would not have surprised Shakespeare. Theatrical extravaganza like *Oliver, Evita, Sweeney Todd* or *Nicholas Nickleby* are the exceptions, and are often to be admired more for their engineering skill than their scenic design. They are very costly; indeed, all sets are, and only the great houses like the National and the Royal Shakespeare, backed as they are by substantial public money, can afford a regular diet of variegated backgrounds.

Television drama thrives on a continuing change of scene. To non-technical viewers (which means practically everyone) the flat two-dimensional screen suggests an affinity with feature films. Decades of cinema going have schooled viewers to expect reality and a fluidity of background, a constant shift of picture.

With multi-camera studio recording, a contained form of shifting background is automatic, in that each camera views the scene from a different angle or distance. But television audiences expect more than a visual tour of one room. A stage play can survive within its single drawing-room set, and the audience will not be upset if they are asked to take the rest of the house for granted.

But television must expand this claustrophobic chamber by the addition of a terrace outside the French windows, a hall with a front door, and a staircase visibly leading up to a bedroom only referred to in the stage play.

Television scripts are almost always written in short scenes which are sometimes no more than a five-second reaction shot of a man sitting alone in a room, a woman staring out of a rain-lashed window; scenes which are only relevant where linked to the scene preceding, and the one following. A television script of 120 pages may include fifty scenes (though not fifty settings) inter-cut with film sequences. Early rehearsals must therefore be fragmented and bitty; later the scenes will merge to make dramatic sense, but at the beginning only the director can have imagined the full end product.

He must do everything to bring the cast into his visual picture. The actors, many of whom may not have been in the pre-filming, must be aware of the whole canvas. There will be a reading of the play with the full cast at first rehearsal. The writer will be there, and time should be allowed for the actors to question him about their parts, and float their own ideas. Television can afford time for discussion.

We are mercifully far from the frenetic conditions of weekly repertory in the theatre, where a full-length play had to be absorbed and learned every seven days — a system that forced the worst of theatrical habits on generations of serious actors. We learned our lines, and picked up the rest of the play as best we could; sometimes it was not until the third performance that the full implication of the plot broke through.

Weekly repertory has gone into limbo, along with that even greater excess — twice nightly repertory; and, incredible to contemplate today, *two* plays a week twice nightly. One play rehearsing Monday, Tuesday and a bit of Wednesday, the other Thursday, Friday and a bit of Saturday. Sundays off.

Patrick Cargill once confessed to me that he had had a spell of this soul-crushing experience. I asked him how on earth he had even managed to learn the lines. He explained that in order to get in two performances every night, the plays had to be cut to the bone, and no one part survived in any volume. Even the most fervent beginner would be reluctant to accept such conditions today; and rightly, for how can one give even the ghost of a performance after two and a half days' rehearsal for a two-hour play?

Actors want guidance. From the oldest theatrical knight to the newest arrival from drama school, they look to the director for decision. They want to be *told*. Once told they will probably argue the toss, but they have small respect for the director without authority. In television, the actor's despair is the director who, in a highly technical medium, elects to work 'off the cuff', relying on a non-existent flair to see him through. In these circumstances, the actor is always the loser, condemned to stand around for hours, waiting for the director to grope his way through to some dim master-plan.

By contrast, no one is more loved than the actor's director, the one who does his homework beforehand, arrives at first rehearsal with his technical decisions firm, and has, in consequence, all the time in the world to devote to the cast and the performances. The actors know they are secure in his hands, and will work all the hours that God sends.

For the unwary newcomer, television can be a technical trap. Daunted by the complexity of the studio hardware, by the urgent need to get pictures on to screen — any pictures — he may drown in technicality, and lose sight of the more enjoyable part of his work, the script and the actors. He does not need to be an electronics expert, but he must understand how to use the machinery. He must know how to get images on to a screen; he must understand cutting, and the reasons for cutting. He must have at least an idea of what his final edit will look like, even if he has no idea how that will be achieved mechanically.

Television drama is hard work, there are no short cuts to success. It demands a plethora of talents, with the old theatrical skills with text and actor augmented by a basic understanding of how to use the sophisticated hardware.

Today's actor is television-wise; he has learned the grammar. As rehearsals progress, he will want to know where the camera is during his speeches, and how close his image will be. He must play to that camera, though not directly, as he would to an audience, if on a very different level. Tell him he is in close-up and he will adjust voice and pitch; if in long shot, pin high to the viewer, he knows he can open out a bit (at the same time wanting to know why he is *not* in close shot). But neither camera nor microphone will accept theatrical bravura. Acting in television is an intimate matter.

Good acting is a blessed balance between natural talent, thought, instinct and technique. Cameras and microphones have sharp eyes and ears, registering the most fleeting expression, the smallest whisper. The television actor must know how to use both.

Whatever else passed them by, the Hollywood stars understood cameras. Many of them were only moderate actors but they were personalities with charisma and a solid film technique. They understood about the size of shots and the importance of angles. They knew about *thinking* their lines before delivering them, or at least how to give an impression of thinking. Many early British films were cast from the theatre, with actors totally inexperienced in film. They were in consequence marred by performances pitched too theatrically. Today, most actors know the difference.

Much of television drama is shot on film, and there will be obvious comparisons between it and the feature film. The most obvious *difference* lies in the composition of the scripts. Broadly speaking, television scripts, even those all on film, have more dialogue than feature films, more words, more speeches.

Feature film enjoys a fluidity that allows the director to shoot all round his subject, cover it from all angles, all distances, to substitute pictures for words; when it comes to editing, he has a mass of images from which to choose.

Time being money, television cannot afford the hours to do this. It is a bulk business, a sausage machine of entertainment, amortising its costs through its quantity and speed of production. The most major television drama film is shot in a matter of weeks, not months. The cinema unit, with only one product to concentrate on, and no urgent television transmission date to meet, can allow itself the luxury of time, within the limits of its budget. Television has, perforce, to substitute words for pictures, particularly in derived work, adaptations of classics and best-selling novels, where the quality of the original dialogue is part of the reason for doing the work at all. It would be difficult to dramatise *Wuthering Heights* or *Anna Karenina* without allowing some of the original Brontë or Tolstoi to creep in, though I can remember several American versions that made determined efforts to achieve this.

Over the years, with a steady increase in filmed content, TV drama has managed to whittle down the words and substitute pictures, but it will probably never match the sparse economy of the good feature film; certainly not for the majority of its output.

Theatre plays, if they are lucky, rehearse on stages. Television drama is less fortunate. Studios are worth their weight in plutonium, are always in demand for recordings, and there is no chance of using them for rehearsal. Nor would there be any particular point, for a bare studio without lights and scenery is no more than a large rehearsal room; whereas a theatre stage is always a stage.

Television drama rehearses in large rooms; in earlier days, in small rooms – used by the BBC – youth clubs, church halls, Territorial Army barracks. One of these last had a large field gun in the middle of the rehearsal space, and everything had to be planned round this immovable monster. All these rooms were smaller than studios, and the sets had to be marked out on the floor in different colours, one on top of the other; which led to confusion amongst actors, and a great deal of walking through solid walls and fireplaces.

It is a confusion not confined to television. Not every actor can imagine the ultimate walls of the set standing up around him. Not every director can, either, which is a great trial to designers.

At drama school we were taught to mime opening and shutting doors – 'to get used to the action'. Rehearsals were full of drama students grasping airy handles, usually on the wrong side of the invisible door.

There is a story about that veteran actor – the late A. E. Matthews – affectionately known as Matty throughout the profession. Matty used to assume a sort of amiable vagueness, an impression of absent-mindedness, that covered a sharp theatrical mind. In his latter years – and he worked on to a great age – he got a reputation for drifting vaguely about the stage, even in performances, suddenly popping up through the wrong door on the wrong side of the stage, to the great astonishment of his fellow actors. But he was so well-loved that everyone put up with it. Well, almost everyone.

There was a new young director, however, who was rehearsing Matty in a stage play. The set had been scrupulously marked out on the empty stage – doors, fireplaces and windows were all indicated. Matty made his first entrance by wandering on through a solid wall. The director's reaction was severe. 'Mr Matthews,' he said sternly. 'I expect my actors to mime the opening and closing of doors. I hope you will do so in future.'

Everyone waited for the world to end. But Matty, after peering vaguely in the direction of the stalls, turned, opened an imaginary door, went through it, and closed it behind him. He then took from his pocket an imaginary piece of paper and wrote on it with his finger. Having folded this invisible note, he stooped and slipped it under the imaginary door.

'What's that?' asked the director, unwisely. 'My resignation,' said Matty; and was only with difficulty persuaded back into the fold.

Much of today's television drama rehearses in custom-built surroundings. The BBC has its own glass and concrete rehearsal block, eighteen studio-sized rooms, with attendant green rooms for actors, canteens and staff rooms. Here sets can be spread out as in the studio, poles mark doors and windows, 'treads' and rostrums create levels, rehearsal properties are sent up from the basement.

Actors like to get used to the properties they will handle in the final recording. The snag about rehearsal properties is that they often bear little relation to the real ones. It is disconcerting for the actor, on arrival into the studio, to find that the two-foot-square kitchen table he has been rehearsing round has turned into an oval mahogany giant, that takes half a minute to circumnavigate and cuts him off from his fellow actors. I mean, how do you lean nonchalantly across four feet of mahogany to kiss the girl of your choice? The toy pistol he has so airily been flourishing in rehearsal now turns out to be a heavy ·455 pistol, too big for any pocket, and extremely tiring to brandish for more than fifteen seconds. The kettle boiling on real gas scalds him, the window blind sticks, and the modest little stairway of the rehearsal room has turned into a majestic spiralling arc.

Nowhere on earth is there anyone more adaptable than the actor. He will cope with anything, if appealed to. The traditional picture of the temperamental actor or actress – rude, selfish, bitchy and impossible – is the exception rather than the rule. They exist, but unless they are very talented indeed, they tend to be avoided.

Most actors are receptive, disciplined and good mannered, ready to adapt, stoical in the face of those disasters and disappointments that stud their lives. It is significant that there are no happy theatrical jokes – they all tell of calamity, about being unemployed for three years, about the other man getting the part, about drying up, failure and public rejection. Only the extraordinary optimism of the profession keeps it going at all.

Every actor is different, every director individual. The good director cherishes his cast, bolsters its morale, calms its astonishing insecurities. The best actors know their worth, but they also know how easily anything theatrical can go wrong, how perilous is the quicksand upon which they move. They know that there is always something more to be got out of a part and are grateful to the director who shows them how.

The process of rehearsing actors in television is basically no different from theatre; it is the same building of lines into scenes, scenes into sequences, sequences into plays. Most actors like to know their 'moves', their theatrical business, before they put down their scripts. In the finicky, accurate confines of television studio recording, they must be made secure in the mechanics of the production. This leaves them free to get on with their performances, which, after all, is what they are there for.

Acting is at once a personal and a team matter. Performances cannot exist for themselves alone; they must feed off each other. It is a process that does not really begin until the lines are learnt, and the scenes begin to move. The wise TV director, having plotted a scene mechanically, will then run it again and again until everyone in it is not only comfortable, but understands precisely what the scene is about. The temptation to push on and give an illusion of brisk progress is seductive, but leaving behind half conceived work is a barren rehearsal practice.

Only the director can judge the overall pacing of a play. Pace is not just going fast or slow, though a variety of tempo is important to drama. One of the failings of much TV drama is that it too often hits an even rhythm throughout, and robs itself of its dramatic potential. Variety of pace is as important as light and shade in acting. It has to do with scenes that are too long and must be cut; or too short, and should be expanded. It has to do with the way information is given to an audience; it is about over-stressing or repetition, indulgent writing and irrelevance. It is about *balance*.

It may even be the mundane matter of actors not picking up their cues quickly enough. Nothing drags a script down more than long meaningful pauses between each speech for no good reason, prolonged silences filled with nothing more interesting than navel contemplation. On days of bad rehearsal (or bad temper) I have been so oppressed by a play's ponderous progress that I have implored the cast, in one all embracing note, to 'get on with it, brisk it up, and knock ten minutes off the running time.' The results were often gratifying; the performances acquired a sparkle absent before. But this was not pacing in the true sense; it was a crude remedy to cure a general torpor that had crept across the production.

Acting is a lonely, unprotected skill. The actor has his talent and his charisma to sell – he has no other real estate, no second line on which to fall back. Either he is good, or he is bad. Worst of all, he is adequate, which promises him nothing better than a sad career of second best.

The immovable director, he who arrives with his script and his thoughts completely locked and refuses to consider any changes, is a dismaying man to work with, unless he happens to be a genius, which is unlikely. Closing one's mind to the intelligence of one's cast is to reject potential excitement. The director must listen to the actor. Nothing is lost if his ideas do not work and have to be abandoned; if good comes of them, it is the director who would be congratulated on thinking of anything so clever.

The lazy director is even more to be dreaded; he who arrives at rehearsal having done no real work and announces blithely that he is going to do it off the top of his head, an almost certain recipe for disaster. This means that he intends to rely on a flow of dramatic inspirations, interspersed with flashes of genius. What actually happens is that he will fool around for days, wasting precious time, and driving everyone mad. The 'moves' he gives the actors will bear small relationship to their dialogue, and none at all to those that will eventually have to be cobbled together in the studio recording. With this regrettable ninny, the actor's traditional patience is once again astounding.

In costume dramas, it helps actors to have some sort of 'mocked-up' rehearsal costumes – long and heavy skirts, armour, awkward hats or boots, etc. It is a bonus for them, and saves a great deal of time and temper when it comes to the recording.

As rehearsal develops, supporting staff will hover round the skirts of the production. The designer, to discuss set changes generated by rehearsal. The film editor, checking the final film edit and its relation to the rest. Costume and make-up artists dropping in to press-gang the cast and bear them off to fittings.

The technical manager (Lighting) will watch progress from the side-lines, marking the movements of the actors, noting their positions on their studio plans. He will enquire closely about lighting cues – a chandelier, switched on, an oil lamp carried up a staircase, the setting of the sun. He will look beyond practicalities, absorb the mood and intention of the scenes, later to match and enhance them with his craft. His colleague in Sound will pop in to pinpoint his own problems. All too rarely, the senior cameraman of the crew may visit, to translate the bare conditions of the rehearsal room into the series of shots that he and his crew will supply in the studio.

There is a time in every drama when further rehearsal would be a mistake. It is not that the piece is perfect – what is? But there is a boiling point, a moment of truth to translate to the studio. Further rehearsal might even be harmful to the play. Ideally, that moment will coincide with the last rehearsal, so that the play moves at the most natural moment.

To the outside world there must seem something suicidal about this transfer to the studio. The change appears brutal, from the assured order of weeks of rehearsal to the frenzied urgency of recording. Here the actors are suddenly enclosed by real walls, thrust into awkward and unbecoming costumes, wigs that make them look absurd. But for actors these are understandable transitions, no more than the progress of a theatre play to its dress rehearsal. What must seem lunacy to the uninitiated is the deliberate fragmentation of a work that has been carefully built up, paced and welded over weeks of work into one perfected whole. The mechanical act of recording chops it into small pieces, so that it might seem (again to the uninitiated) that the play had gone back to its first days of rehearsal. It is, of course, an illusion.

When television was live, drama had to be run in one piece. At eight o'clock somebody shouted 'Go' and at nine-thirty you faded down on the last caption of a ninety-minute play. With any luck, not too much would have gone wrong – a few fluffs from the actors, a couple of microphones in shot, that nasty moment when two cameras ran into each other. Now drama is recorded scene by scene, often as it goes along. Everyone in television expects this, except for the occasional greyhead who mourns the 'good old days of live TV'.

As one who had to act and direct in those good old days, I can tell you how glad I was when recording became the norm.

The inexperienced television actor, thrust overnight into the hubbub of his first studio, might feel some dismay that the director who has been so sympathetic in rehearsal has now abandoned him. Now the attention has moved to the cameramen peering into their view-finders, the sound operators swinging their booms over the actors' heads and occasionally making contact; to the electricians staring discontentedly up at lamps; with property men hanging last-minute curtains. The actor might feel that his importance to the play, so evident in rehearsal, is now secondary to the costume designer darting into the set to tweak his Napoleonic epaulettes, or the beautiful make-up girl peering impersonally at his wig. The scenes, so flowing in rehearsal, now limp through, constantly interrupted to accommodate the director's visual dreams. When the moment finally comes to run the scene, the actor's sonorous tones are drowned by a band of carpenters correcting the wobble on a bannister rail. His friendly director is largely invisible, glimpsed briefly as he flits down from the control gallery to set up a shot, or discuss an obstinate shadow on the leading lady's face. He is clearly too busy to spare the actor more than an abstracted glance before darting back to more important things in the gallery.

This abrupt shift in concentration is inevitable. It is therefore essential that the actor enters the studio with his performance so solid, that nothing can chip its quality.

The studio is under the control of the production assistant (sometimes called the production manager). He has been the director's right-hand man (or woman, for women are particularly good assistants) throughout preparation, location shooting, rehearsal and now recording. It is a heavy responsibility. He must maintain studio discipline with crews that spend their lives in such conditions, as opposed to his particular drama unit, for which it is an occasion.

He must be a firm and genial tactician, encouraging, coaxing, chiding, praising, compromising, and always authoritative. His duties range from persuading carpenters to knock in three-inch nails silently to keeping his director's nose to the recording grindstone. To aid him, he has an assistant floor manager, who has been with him throughout production; script in hand, he or she works with the cast, keeping them aware of progress, ready for the next scene. With him are the property men and visual effects; and, at all times, liaising with the production assistant himself. There is also a floor assistant – in television terms a sort of glorified callboy/girl, who works to the PA and keeps the cast comfortable and coming. This floor assistant might well have been a deputy stage manager in the theatre, so keen is the queue to enter television drama.

The production assistant balances the urgent need to get on with the recording with infuriating but necessary delays – adjustments to lighting, sets, costume changes, actors who mysteriously disappear for excellent reasons. The settings and the lighting (or a great part of them) should be ready for the actors when they arrive, but there will always be fine adjustments during the studio days. Everyone wants perfection, and there is only a limited time to achieve it.

As television has sophisticated itself, the expectations of studio productivity have changed. For years the yardstick was to obtain thirty minutes of programme per day from a studio, live or recorded, a legacy from some convention long forgotten by everyone. But television has compounded its complications and this has got steadily harder to achieve; many fifty-minute drama scripts now require three studio days for recording. Longer plays have time in proportion, but anything above six days is a television luxury. Even with the expansion, it remains an operation of extraordinary speed and efficiency, unique to television drama.

Running over the allotted studio time allowed is a crime that furrows the brow of the television planner. Useless to protest that the studio caught fire, that the roof fell in. The official view is that a production must complete. There is already another programme waiting inexorably outside the studio doors.

That said, a 100 per cent immaculate record is a pipe-dream. Making dramas is not manufacturing plastic buckets. The work is special, and emotional, vulnerable to disaster. (So presumably are plastic bucket production lines, but somehow this is harder to be passionate about.) Most dramas are completed faithfully in the given time, though often by the skin of their on-the-spot ingenuity, by last-minute cutting and reshaping. Serials have the flexibility of knocking on an uncompleted scene to the next episode's recording session, provided that particular set can reappear in the studio. But plays have no such leeway.

There are legitimate reasons for non-completion. Systems fail, cameras break down. There are late starts, brought about by everything from a sudden union meeting to a traffic jam on the North Circular Road. Less legitimately, it may be discovered at this late stage that the whole conception is too ambitious to be achieved in the time; there is little excuse for this for ample preparation time is allowed to avoid this crisis. Drama, in its run-up period, is surrounded by experts, and it is reasonable to assume that every conceivable complication has been encountered before.

It is always possible, though mercifully it does not happen often, that the director himself may not be up to the technical challenge. He may be an excellent drama director, firm about what he is trying to achieve visually, but without the experience to get it on to the screen. Then the producer in the gallery, and the production assistant on the studio floor, will have to step in and nurse him forward, guiding him to the shots and effects he is striving after; yet one more chore for the assistant, who always seems to rise to the occasion.

Television lighting has reached a peak of perfection that often matches that of the cinema, at a fraction of the time and cost. Major dramas are allowed a separate 'set and light' day, and this at least allows the technical manager to work unfidgeted by the feeling that he is holding up the recording every time he wants to alter the angle of a lamp. But it is little enough time for what has to be done.

Like the new theatres, modern television studios have magnificent lighting equipment. Subtleties unknown twenty years ago are a matter of course today: low key lighting, deliberate pools of darkness, soft light reflected from white sheets hung in fronts of sets – the whole being regulated by consoles of computer efficiency.

Like the direction of the play, the lighting is never complete. There is no moment in a recording session when the technical manager is not running up and down the steep steps between gallery and studio, to add or subtract. He is part of the production from its birth, and fruitful partnerships grow between him and the director; and, of course, the designer, for each enhances the skills of the other.

If the production assistant is in charge of the studio, the total responsibility stays with the director, working between the studio and the gallery, the nerve centre of the operation. From here he will generate the whole spirit and impetus of the session, supported by his producer. He is surrounded by experts. His director's assistant (a secretary with responsibilities far beyond those of the ordinary secretary) is at his elbow, final recording script before her, timing, noting changes and 'takes', storing up information for the final edit. All shots in a television drama are numbered, so that when the assistant calls the shot numbers, as she does throughout, everyone in the studio knows where he is.

At the director's other elbow sits the vision mixer, who has the memory of an elephant and eyes that can watch six monitors at once, each displaying the current picture held by the studio cameras. It is his or her job, with the director's instruction, to cut or mix from one picture to the next. Further down the 'desk' sits a second technical manager, in charge of the actual recording operation. Tucked away in a corner is the operator who will feed in any technical trickeries, 'laid-in' backgrounds, 'wipes', electronic captions, and other wizardries. Spread around the gallery will be make-up artists critically inspecting their work on camera, and costume designers tut-tutting over actors mis-wearing their costumes; and, of course, the designer himself, making sure that his dreams come true.

There have always been the politest of controversies between designer and director as to what is being seen, or not seen, on the screen – the designer determined that not a foot of his scenery will be missed, the director more anxious to look at his actors. How well I remember that prompting voice from the back of the gallery: 'If you could just pan up a bit, you could see the frieze – it's absolutely typical of the period . . .' or: 'I give you a genuine crystal chandelier, and so far all we've seen is a three-second flash of it . . .'

Idle to protest that whilst inspecting friezes and admiring chandeliers, we are missing actors saying vital things. That chandelier is the centre-piece of the designer's conception.

Adjacent to the central gallery position, separated only by glass, is the lighting area, controlling the studio lighting by console, setting up cues, balancing the quality and intensity of the pictures. On the other side of central control, a similar compartment devoted to the sound supervisor and his staff. Here are collected all the sounds and speeches that come up from the studio, including visitors tripping over camera cables, to be balanced and stored up for the editing; from here, too, can be fed in additional sound, music and effects, by tape or disc. Though today many such 'spot' effects are dubbed on afterwards in the post-production process.

All three compartments are in touch with the studio, where the production assistant, the cameramen and sound operators wear headphones and can hear everything that originates from the gallery – including the occasional passionate bursts of language that flow down from the harassed director. Amongst his other talents, the production assistant must know how to translate the most blistering message into soothing terms. So that 'Tell that silly bitch, for the very last time, to get on her sodding marks . . .' emerges in the studio as 'Mary, darling, just a little more to your left, sweet . . .'

The actual rhythm of recording depends on the customs and practice of the particular organisation. It was once confined to one session at the end of the final studio day, a fifty-minute episode being given two and a half hours' recording time, longer plays in proportion. At the time this seemed generous. One was encouraged to keep going, stopping only for such emergencies as fire, the total collapse of the set, or death.

The increased ambitions of producers and directors, and the more sophisticated use of the medium by writers, have all helped to make 'rehearse-record' general. Scenes are rehearsed thoroughly, then recorded whilst they are 'hot'. The long live transmission imposed a tremendous strain on cameramen, sound operators, vision mixers, the director, everyone on the production team. Actors, who would make light of a full-length play in the theatre, found the unfamiliar television operation an exhausting marathon; from which they did not always emerge the winners.

There is no going back, even if anyone wanted to. Yet I am still asked if it would not be better to return to live television drama. 'Actors loved it,' I am assured. 'It got their adrenalin going.' I acted in a lot of live television, and I can tell you that actors *didn't* love it – they accepted it because there was no other way. It was a chancy, one-off operation, with no hope of retrieving your mistakes. I simply do not believe that performances were better then. Why should they have been? Actors will always give their best at all times, whatever the conditions.

There are many stages between literal 'rehearse-record', which requires recording facilities linked to the studio throughout the session, and is thus, in the jargon of planning, 'unreasonably resource-consuming', and more moderate versions of the mode. There can be 'rehearse-record' for fixed intervals – from three o'clock every afternoon, or each evening. Some form of 'rehearse-record' is now inevitable. It has given television drama a technical standard that no one would willingly abandon. In the end, it is no more than a tape version of filming, except that in filming every single shot is 'rehearse-record', whilst the studio secures complete scenes in one take.

The new fluidity of the system allows drama to record out of sequence. If a play has, say, three scenes in the House of Commons – one at the beginning of the play, one in the middle, and one at the end – it would be lunacy to record them in the order in which they appear in the script, over a series of days, with a small army of MP extras eating their heads off at the production's expense. The three scenes must be recorded in one session. If this creates extra editing, it saves other costs, and a great deal of hanging about and inconvenience. The scenes completed, the cumbersome House of Commons can be bundled out into the night, and something else substituted for the following day. Such a pity one cannot threaten the real House with the same treatment, unless it behaves better.

Recordings are built up, scene by scene. If there are errors, technical or artistic, the scene is retaken. Time and bad luck are the enemies. A small mechanical breakdown can threaten completion; indecision on the part of the director can compound the disaster. Management has never been slow to inform drama that 'You cannot afford these selfish directors who perpetually run over time.' Drama's answer has its own logic: 'They are often the best directors . . .'

Of course there is an element of blackmail to it. Once nine tenths of *Hamlet* has been recorded, it is a brave management that will abandon the last tenth, and so the whole production. Extra time is found, somehow, and the director good enough to be doing *Hamlet* is unlikely to be disconcerted by dark mutterings from the management. He knows he will be asked back.

The majority of television directors are freelance, working where they will, BBC or ITV, in film or theatre, making commercials and small fortunes. They can hardly be expected to nurture a particular loyalty to any one organisation, or weep for a planner who has had to accept yet one more studio over-run. Considering the huge mass of drama recorded every year, the regrettable occasions are few enough, and the results make the fuss worthwhile.

Studio recording is instant film making, on tape. Each unit is required to complete a fifty, seventy-five, or ninety-minute 'film' in a matter of hours. Even after my many years in television, it still remains to me a recurring miracle, achieved by energy and enthusiasm, never to be taken for granted. Like any visit to the theatre I find in it the magic that clings to all theatrical occasions.

The play, the series or serials episode, is now completed. But it exists only in fragments. The scenes recorded on location have been transferred to tape and added to the rest. The drama is now a row of tins. It has to be assembled.

10

Post-Production

Post-production is the last stage of the dramatic journey. It is the considered assembly of all the material that has been shot, location or studio. It is selection, adjustment, smoothing out, completion.

The earliest films were editorially crude. The camera was switched on, viewing much the same as the eye of a playgoer in the tenth row of the stalls, and the actors were signalled to get on with the acting. The picture was static, the cast moving in and out of frame as directed. There were few changes of angle, and fewer close-ups, though directors like D. W. Griffith hit on the idea of vignetting part of the whole picture to create the idea of close-up. But some editing was unavoidable; the end of one scene had to be joined to the beginning of the next.

But even in silent films, uncomplicated by the problems of sound, editors and directors soon became ambitious. They began to shuffle the visual pack, chopping up takes and scenes, interposing them with each other. This was a true artistic advance – the realisation that the story could be better told and emphasised by even simple editing.

When sound arrived, post-production grew mightily. It was not merely the marvel of voices in dialogue; behind them there had to be all the natural sounds of life – traffic, wind, sea, armies on the march, gunfire rumbling. There had to be spot effects; telephones ringing and doors slamming, sounds that could be recorded on the spot, but might afterwards need grading – heightened or reduced.

Many early film scenes, particularly the exteriors, depended heavily on dubbing. The early film makers distrusted direct sound on location. They clung to the control that studios gave to production, and pre-war films were full of improbably and falsely lit exterior scenes – woods and fields that reeked of backcloths and imitation grass. Scenes shot on location had their dialogue dubbed in after-wards, even the most prolonged sequences. So, too, was the specially composed music, matched and timed to a frame.

Television got the benefit of years of feature film experiment; it inherited a highly sophisticated editing system. Most post-war tele-vision drama was live, and only the rare filmed programmes – of any sort – needed post-production. If inserts for a crime series were pre-filmed, they would be edited and fed into the mainstream of the transmission as it occurred. It was a hair-raising business, cueing the film at the exact moment to run through its ten-second leader and arrive on the screen at the exact moment. It only needed the actor to fumble the dialogue, or leave something out to upset the visual applecart. Many an artist has been left staring open-mouthed in close-up, waiting through eternity for the film picture to arrive. We became very good at inventing 'fill-in' business to cover these catastrophes.

The budgets for my first serials were so small that, to save money, I used to film without sound at all, covering the unnatural silences of the action sequences with loud music. Enthusiastic sound super-visors would augment this by dropping in extra effects as the trans-mission went out – rivers gurgling, seagulls, traffic. It seemed to work well then. It would look and sound quite awful today.

As far as film editing and dubbing went the work had already been done for television. It had only to adopt the experience of the cinema. It wasn't long before the volume of television film – the sheer mileage of film stock – was far greater than that of the com-bined British film industry, but the work cycles were identical: rushes with synchronised sound, pictures and sound for editing, the pre-ferred takes identified, the final agreed cut sent off for negative cutting by the laboratories, the 'answer' prints, the final prints, the grading for overall quality, and the final dubbing and smoothing out by post-production. The only difference was the pace of it all. Tele-vision is a fast medium; it accelerates all its processes, editing and post-production amongst them.

The cinema had made editing almost as important a contribution as that of the writer and director. It accepted that it was a sensitive art, mechanically applied. The final print, altered, shortened, length-ened, regrouped and at last agreed, is run through in a dubbing theatre, with all the dialogue and natural sound selected from its making: to this is added new sound, from a complex of separate film tracks, pre-prepared and accurately timed. It may be augmented background noises, spot effects, or incidental music. Dubbing is a manipulation; sound may be manoeuvred to overlap from one scene to another, its volume relative to each. Dialogue may be added or substituted, by actors in front of microphones working to lip-synchronisation of the pictures run before them.

It is an operation of exact timings, governed by 'cue-sheets' that are the Bibles of the sessions. These are minute appreciations of all the information that is to be added, or manipulated, during post-production, its timing, its intensity, it spreads between scenes. The dubbing editor, like the film editor, is part of the artistic team, and his contribution may mean the difference between very good and excellent.

Film stock in television (nearly always 16mm) runs to millions of feet every year, most of which has to be processed, printed, viewed and selected. Keeping track of it all is a profession in itself – an unlabelled can of film is lost without trace for ever; identification becomes even more essential as these miles of film are chopped into smaller and smaller segments, as takes are approved or rejected or, as so often happens, are put aside 'just in case'.

No prudent editor gets rid of anything still remotely usable. Every 'trim' – even a couple of seconds – is hung on a rack, in case the unpredictable director changes his mind. Every cutting room has its sad tale of the lost take, discarded into some overflowing bin of junked film (but which one?), which is later the subject of bitter recriminations all round.

Rough cuts are the first assembly of scenes that may look something like the end-product; they may not be 'finely' edited, in the sense of film exactitude, and many of the cutting points – say, the end of a scene – will be prolonged to allow discussion and choice. Opticals – dissolves, the slow melding of one picture into another to denote the passing of time or space, fades-down or up, freeze frames when the action is halted, slow-motion sequences – can be discussed later, timed to the exact moment (say the beginning and end of a dissolve) and sent off to the laboratories for special processing.

The editing of *film* presented no particular challenge to television, beyond that of coping with the huge amount. The rules had been worked out years before.

Then tape recording arrived, and with it a new craft; though, in truth, it was no more than a new way of producing the same results. Two-inch tape was the recording stock, the edited film inserts being transferred to the same studio tape.

In the fifties, tape editing seemed very difficult. Rumour hinted at appalling problems with sound and picture, and we were discouraged from creating unnecessary edits. This was editing at its simplest, the plain cutting and joining of sequences: a tedious business, giving scant opportunity for second thoughts, and increasing the risk of physical disturbances at the joins when the tape was transmitted. The fact that sound and picture were o·6 seconds apart on the one tape tended to compromise exact editing points.

But the system at least worked. Drama was recorded in large segments, sometimes half the play. It was not uncommon, in the sixties, for the director and editor to sit down after the recording and edit the production there and then. Most of it was simple 'butt' joins, one scene to the next, and a few trims and shortenings. I cannot recall any of it taking very long. But if we could see those recordings now, we would find a lot wrong with them, and itch to turn our hands to re-editing.

The equipment was basic – one machine editing, with no elaborate tape dubbing suites. The material you had to work with was the tape you had built up from recording and location.

In contrast to the total fluidity of film editing, tape editing was cumbersome and restrictive. One could not *add* to the whole as with film, where scenes shot from every angle and point of view were there to be juggled and juxtapositioned. Nor could one hold the tape up to the light to check the picture (nor can one today, but there is no longer the necessity). One could, of course, move scenes in relation to each other, shorten them, eliminate them altogether. But it was stiffly inflexible; and, as such, frustrating, for the temptation to improve is irresistible. No one has ever run through a final edit without seeing something more to be done.

The system's advantages spurred its improvement. Today's tape editing is as flexible as for film. It is achieved without physical cutting, the editing being done between two videotape machines working in unison. One machine holds the recorded material, the other slowly builds up the final version from it, taking only selected scenes and sequences. The transfer from one machine to another is exact and rapid. If tape opticals are required – say, a slow dissolve – a third machine is brought into use, and the optical created by the same system of transference.

Tape dubbing suites are masterpieces of streamlined ingenuity. Multiple 'tracks', as in film, can be pre-prepared and fed into the master tape with the accuracy of a single frame. Sounds can be balanced, effects and music added and timed. New dialogue can be introduced.

What is the magic that makes one piece of editing dull and the other exciting? What is a good editor? The bad one is easy enough to identify, but definitions of quality are always suspect. Good editing, like good directing, is more than mechanics. It's not just sticking one bit of stock to another, or dropping in the occasional reaction shot. Editing has to be felt – it is an understanding of the values of a scene, its tension, its despairs and exhilarations, all to be enhanced by a deft manipulation of the images. Editing is knowing how long a shot can be held, or the exact moment to cut away from a reaction. It can never be arithmetical. The great editors have a dramatic taste that chimes with that of the director.

As tape editing increased, it became urgent to find a way of identifying exact moments in the huge rolls of tape, down to a frame; to pinpoint that desired moment and produce it instantly.

The answer was Time Code. This system postulates that all recording timings are identified in *real* time – by the twenty-four-hour clock – so that any moment in the script is pinpointed by that actual hour, minute, second and part second. The line of dialogue recorded at nineteen hundred hours twenty-eight minutes and seventeen seconds will be so registered by the Time Code, which prints the real time numerals on the tape.

The director's assistant, when she wishes to make a note about any incident in the recording, marks the actual time against it in the script, knowing that identical time is being printed on the tape. This simplification is used throughout all drama editing and post-production.

Time Code has streamlined editing, making it unnecessary to plough through miles of tape in quest of an elusive take; unwanted footage can be spooled through rapidly to the required point.

Most dramas are recorded simultaneously on cassettes which are also Time Coded. These are invaluable to the director, allowing him to work out in advance roughly what he will do in his main editing. He can discard bad takes, decide cutting points, freeze the frame to consider split seconds. He can do it without the pressure of feeling that he is holding up the entire editing session whilst he thinks. It is a facility that saves precious time, though there is a pessimistic view in management that it merely encourages directors to think up many more cuts and edits than they would otherwise have done. I find this view depressing. No director is going to leave things in the tape that he does not like, whatever the editing circumstances, or however pressed for time.

The production assistant may prepare the first rough cut, or the editor himself may assemble it from script and notes. Either way, director and editor are in partnership from that point. Running a rough cut a few times is a sure way of finding the weaknesses in the recording. The director may find it very different from his first imaginings; it may be slower. It may make its points laboriously. It may not make them at all. It may be monotonous. On the other hand, it may turn out to be exciting beyond all expectations.

Fine editing (as opposed to rough) cures a lot of ills. Scenes can be clipped, shots transposed, a variation of pace at least suggested. Even bad performances, suspected in rehearsal but persevered with, may have to be radically reduced. The old complaint of the film actor that his performance was left on the cutting room floor is no myth. It happens, and not always because of a bad performance. Sometimes it is because it is too good, and is stealing the scenes from the star. More creditably, it may be because the film is too long, and something has to go. It occurs all too often in feature films, but is less frequent, and less brutal, in television.

Once the final edit has been agreed, and the opticals arranged for, the last stage of production has been reached – dubbing, and the finishing gloss.

Twenty years of television drama has seen sharp changes. From the live play done, of necessity, in one piece, through the early recordings still made in one block, it has arrived at a studio situation where the multi-camera system is in danger of being eroded. On tape-location it has developed from a four camera to a two camera, and now frequently to a single camera, operation. In the studio several cameras are still used on each set, but the tendency is to tackle only one scene at a time and then break the recording, possibly adding a few extra close-ups and reverse shots as luxuries at the end of the scene.

In these circumstances the other cameramen might as well park their cameras for the night and go home, for there is little need for them. If they are used at all, it is only to spread the load diplomatically amongst the whole crew.

The practice has created a mass demand for tape editing and post-production, the efficiency of which has encouraged directors to rely on it automatically; on the principle that what wasn't obtained in the studio can always be added in the dubbing suite. Managements, already short of editing facilities, and conscious of the cost of new equipment, predict darkly that the whole studio operation will soon be reduced to a one camera operation. I am more optimistic. It happens on occasion, but for financial reasons alone, the bulk of television drama must still be shot multi-camera, at the brisk pace that is television's production advantage.

Post-production completed, it only remains to ensure a perfect quality transmission film or tape, free from technical blemishes, colour graded throughout. Visual defects irritate the viewer and may turn his attention to something else; 'something else', in television, usually means the opposition.

The moment when nothing more can be done to a production is one of great emotional satisfaction; and of regret, too, that the work and its partnerships is over. The viewer may only appreciate one tenth of the tiny adjustments and subtleties that have gone into the whole programme. But the *sum* of those adjustments may have made the difference between success and failure.

The work, so long a private creation between writer, producer, director, actor, designer and technician, must now, for an hour or two, become the property of the public; for their enjoyment, their delight – and their verdict.

11

The Responsibilities of Television

Between the World Wars, the European dictators used radio propaganda remorselessly to establish their ideologies. Radio had already demonstrated its power as a mass means of entertainment and education. It was the obvious tool for unscrupulous men, intent on national power and international conquest. It is no coincidence that, over the past fifty years, any rebellion seeking to overthrow the established power has moved first to capture the means of communication – the radio stations and, latterly, the television centres.

Television, with its instant mixture of words and pictures, is the most powerful communicator in history. It can be used unscrupulously for the destruction of truth, and the substitution of one's own version of it. We can be thankful that so many countries and governments have refused to allow it to become the instrument of partisan politics. In Britain, there is a great deal of political reportage, discussions and interviews, most of which is boring to an unparalleled degree. But the screen time is parcelled out between the major political parties, who no doubt have their stop-watchdogs, counting every second of their opponents' screen time. There are countries, so often those emerging into a new and unfamiliar independence, that have been unable to resist the temptation to use television to consolidate their regimes; and, in doing so, have not always been fastidious about the truth.

Happily, it is not all one way. Television itself is formidable. The camera has a cold eye for insincerity and falsehood. Even uncertainty and ignorance are magnified, sometimes unfairly, into shiftiness. In today's television-wise world, politicians and unions leaders, industrialists and authorities of all kinds are endlessly interviewed. Time and time again, rather than admit ignorance, they are betrayed into instant answers that are either meaningless or evasive. Experience has now bred in them an awareness of danger, and a determination to say nothing that can be misconstrued – a depressing surrender of truth to expediency. How often do politicians, when asked a direct if difficult question about the parlous condition of the Health Service, take refuge in the formula: 'Before I answer that question, I would like to remind you of the disgraceful record of the last Government in this area . . .' Their political grandfathers were free from this strain. They were spared the necessity of the dashing to a radio or television studio to justify their every decision to a bored public. Nor did they rush frantically around the world, giving interviews at every stage of their journeys. They sat at home, and allowed themselves time for thought.

Up to a couple of centuries ago, a mere pause in time, the fastest pace at which information could be spread was that of a man on a horse (unless one includes those enigmatic Indian smoke signals, which must have given rise to grave misinterpretation). There were few newspapers, no means of distributing them rapidly, and not all that many people to read them when they arrived. News spread through from town to town, village to village, and it probably took days for the remoter hamlets of Britain to hear the result of the Battle of Waterloo, a delay that would make small difference to their lives. Napoleon was beaten – the date was hardly important.

Nowadays facts are known as they occur, and only books, which have to be read and therefore take time, remind us of a more pedestrian way of getting information.

Television is flooded with facts; not merely news, though this is available round the clock. There are discussions and confrontations and explanations, panels of experts, current affairs programmes, phone-ins, access programmes, on-the-spot interviews everywhere from Park Avenue to Pakistan. Fingers wag at us remorselessly from the screen, telling us how to live, what to admire, what to buy, eat and drink; at election time, how to vote and why. No television service is complete without its pundits, whose every word is law.

There are those who insist that the prime purpose of television is immediacy. I believe that it has other equally prime purposes, amongst them entertainment. A diet of stark fact would soon give the viewer indigestion. Certainly there must be room for good journalism and current affairs. Television news reportage has a high standard of responsibility. The best of current affairs programmes are important and instructive; the worst are crude 'pull togethers' of stale information, more culpable than any bad fictional programme in that they purport to deal with the truth.

Reporting plain fact is straightforward enough; analysing it and its importance requires a cool and equable stance. Pure documentary is a clear-cut matter. It is the unbiased presentation of true facts and situations; it is the word spoken, the action committed, the decisions taken. It is what actually happened. If the documentary wishes to speculate, it must allow time for opposing opinions. If it reconstructs events, using actors and scripted scenes, it must indicate clearly what is simulation, and what is not.

Even the most careful simulation can rob the documentary of its 'purity'. The account of a notorious murder trial may be scrupulous in using only the words spoken by judge, counsel, witnesses and accused. It may add no more than a top-and-tail commentary, and a few linking comments between the days of the trial. But the very act of recreating the scene, in a courtroom peopled by actors, invites a bending of the truth. Murder trials are often tedious, full of longueurs and repetitions. To make the programme acceptable in length, and palatable to the impatient viewer, there may have to be cuts which automatically revalue the actual course of events, boring as this may have been. Even the unconscious bias of an intelligent actor, who has never agreed with official verdict, may slant his performance of the eminent QC who gained it. I remember a film about that arch-villain Adolf Hitler in which, in the hands of a most skilful actor, the character of the dictator became more and more sympathetic as destiny closed in upon him. In the final scenes in the Berlin bunker, one was actually *sorry* for the man; what a pity it was that it all had to end so badly for him!

Even the most responsible drama documentary (of which more later) can never have the truth of real reportage. Drama is the art of spoof and illusion. It tidies life up, cuts through the boring bits, and highlights the excitements.

It telescopes time. It can take, for example, the last meeting of a wife and husband before separation (which in life would be full of sullen recriminations and silences) and reshape it into a cut-and-thrust of deft speeches which build on each other and end in a dramatic exit for the husband and a flurry of bitter tears for the wife. Life is rarely so neat – it is notoriously sloppy, and it is up to drama to remodel its truths. The most stark script gives only an illusion of reality. What emerges may be magnificent drama, moving, even improving. But nothing will make it reportage.

Nor is this a cause for dismay. A world without story-telling would be a dull place. One of the first signs that a tribe is settling down to a secure and continuing mode of life is the emergence of myths and legends; which, as the settlement of the tribe progresses, will be converted into dramatic, acted-out versions of the tribal history. Drama appeals to the emotions, touching heart and gut; to accomplish which it overstresses (or understresses) as it thinks fit, cuts and adds to suit its purpose. It is as essential to the health of television as to life itself.

That drama is fiction in no way releases its producers from responsibility. One cannot hide behind that convenient old shield, 'It's only a play . . .' Television penetrates the heart of peoples' lives – the home. It bids fair to become the king of the Englishman's castle. It is a fatally easy form of entertainment. A visit to the theatre or the cinema is an occasion. One must move from one's home, travel distances, meet friends for a drink before or a meal afterwards. One sits in a theatrical ambience, with hundreds of strangers, facing an acting area that pretends to be nothing else. One may be entranced, outraged, moved – but one is never in doubt of the formality of the occasion.

By contrast, television drama is a domestic matter, with the family in attendance – or part attendance, for the rigours of family life work against uninterrupted viewing.

The moments of truth of any play are often lost in telephone calls, children's demands, or the unwelcome appearance of an earnest young man from an obscure religious sect at the front door.

If a play offends it is an assault within the home and its outrage is the greater. Television invades man's privacy to an extent he would not tolerate from friend or neighbour. Drama, traditionally the host of the evening's entertainment, is now the guest in the house. As such, it should assume the graces and responsibilities of a guest.

The drama maker's first responsibility is to make good drama; and one assumes that even the most perverse director does not set out deliberately to make a bad production. But nothing is certain in play-making, and things go wrong in television, as they do in the theatre, the cinema and in books. There are unbelievable paintings at most exhibitions, our landscapes are scarred with bad architecture.

Drama's responsibility is an old one. It is to do with dramatic content and its presentation, with the intentions of writer and director. It is to do with those Four Horsemen of the Television Apocalypse – Violence, Sex, Swearing and Blasphemy. For three decades I have been on committees examining the effect of these four on the viewer, particularly the young. Their findings have usually been no more than reiteration of those same commonsense philosophies held by serious programme makers since television began – rules, frequently unwritten, which exist in all television organisations; it would be unthinkable if they did not. But in the end I put a greater trust on personal taste, commonsense, and a producer's regard for *all* viewers who might reasonably be expected to be watching at the hour of his transmission. One should be able to assume, for example, that children of five will not be glued to the television set at eleven o'clock at night. It happens, but how can anyone cater for that lunatic fringe of irresponsible parents?

Let's take our Four Horsemen one by one, and consider how they may best be corralled. In a visual medium violence registers under two headings: first, the way in which it is presented; second, the intention of the director in presenting it at all. Violence is more than rough action, fights, hard blows, even murder or death. All these can fill the screen and leave no sense of outrage or unease. There are better definitions: my own is that violence is the unnecessary addition and stressing of violent images in a script, actions that do not spring naturally from the story and its characters. Actions which, far from forwarding the drama, actually halt it whilst we experience a gratuitous emphasis on cruelty and pain. This is the violence that viewers challenge, though they may not be able to explain why.

The director's production intentions must be clear. If he has determined from the start that the script will be violent, pandering to that viewing coterie that has had its sensitivities blunted to the point of confusing vicarious pain with entertainment, then that director is about to make a bad programme. Violence for violence's sake is a poor sort of art.

Presentation is as important as content. Violent actions need not automatically offend. A simple incident from a Western illustrates this. An Indian waits behind a rock in the Arizona desert to shoot a cowboy riding through the ravine below. He fires, the cowboy pitches from his horse, dead or wounded according to his importance to the script. A scene from twenty thousand Westerns, that could not distress the youngest viewer. But let the eye of the camera move in with the bullet (with a super-swift zoom) and, in close shot, see it enter the cowboy with all the disgusting physical details of a large bullet exploding within a human body, and the viewer will be outraged. Yet he has witnessed precisely the same action – it is only the presentation that has differed. Each of us has his threshold of acceptance, beyond which our instinct forbids us to go, but here the disgust would be universal, for the eye has been brought to bear too *closely* on agony and physical disintegration.

There is no such problem in the theatre, where every play is seen in continuing long shot. But the camera has the power to rub our noses in its images. Is a film ever improved by a close-up of blood and brains spilling out of a crushed skull? Are we dramatically better for a close, prolonged view of a martyr burning at the stake? Isn't our imagination powerful enough to feel the suffering?

The duration that a shot is held may be as important as the shot itself. If the camera lingers too long on a cruel action, there must grow in the sensitive viewer an uncomfortable feeling that he is meant to be enjoying the agony. The director has lingered deliberately. The same director, by the same wrong-headed instinct, will probably return again and again to that shot, as if he (and therefore the viewer) could not get enough of the horror.

These two cornerstones – presentation and intention – are not necessarily related. Going over the violent top may be the result of inexperience rather than a sinister sadism in the director. He may have convinced himself that, in order to push home the moral of his drama, he must show the pain to be overwhelming. Experience would have told him that precisely the same effect could have been gained subtly; and if experience didn't, his producer should have.

It is the ultimate absurdity to shock the viewer to the point where he switches off. Drama without an audience is pointless, and no television writer, producer or director can afford to ignore the particular make-up of his audience. It has not the organic strength of the theatre audience, deliberately assembled for enjoyment at all costs. The viewer, literally on home ground, may be watching by chance – he just happened to switch on at that moment. He has caught the opening of your play, and with any luck will stay with it. But there are other diversions bidding for his attention, and it is fatally easy for him to switch off or over, through irritation or boredom. A fair percentage of the television audience is of a roving character. Once won, it has to be held.

There is a more captive audience, to whom television has become something of a blessing; the elderly, who don't feel like venturing out on a wild night; the pensioner, who can't afford to; the lonely, living on the outskirts of a remote village, or in the even greater loneliness of a bed-sitter in a large city; the young married couple who cannot easily get out when their children are babies or tots; whole families on festive occasions – Christmas, Easter, bank holidays. Above all, the children, who are offered a magical range of entertainment, from cartoons to educational documentaries.

Television is a fine teacher. A thirty-minute visual tour of Ethiopia will tell a classroom more than hours of book-bound geography, and make it enjoyable. The physical world, its problems and peoples, its customs and contours, is there for the turn of a switch. Series like David Attenborough's splendid *Life on Earth* or, some years before, Kenneth Clark's *Civilization*, are storehouses of information, served up in digestible chunks. Dramatised documentaries like *The Fight Against Slavery* or *The Voyage of Charles Darwin* illuminate corners of history for a vast new audience. The makers of these factual blockbusters carry a proportionate responsibility; a fact wrong, a fact omitted for the best of reasons, may be taken as a bending of the truth, to suit the programme and its authors.

Recognising the need for responsibility, we must ask ourselves what would happen if we were irresponsible. If villainy, immorality and deceit were seen to prosper unchecked in every drama, would general wickedness multiply? The long tradition in drama is that the wicked should not win. Samuel Johnson approved of Nahum Tate's appalling rewrite of *King Lear* (which banished the Fool and allows both Lear and Cordelia to survive) because Shakespeare's version permitted the triumph of evil over good. The early Film Censors were adamant that the villain should always be seen to get his come-uppance. I don't know how much hard research they did before making their stern rulings, but they were operating in an age of entertainment considerably less permissive than our own, and they were taking no chances with public morals.

How great is the danger of corruption from fictional television? TV drama is young – in today's sophisticated form, very young. The committees and experts and television academics (who proliferate with the years) who examine the effects of the medium on the viewer are usually strong on philosophy and short on hard evidence.

Television sponsors a lot of audience research. Hundreds of viewers are tackled each week, asked what programmes they watched, for how long, and how they liked them. But these casual enquiries (casual in the true research sense) yield information that is more general than specific.

It is easy to record mechanically whether a TV set was switched on between six in the evening and midnight. It is more difficult to prove how many people were watching it all that time, or whether half of them watched at all. Sets play to empty rooms. Door-to-door and street enquiries, though personal, are still rough and ready – stock questions often encourage stock answers; and from a few hundred such enquiries springs an automatic assumption that fifteen million viewers have followed the programme; a reckoning that can surely not be accurate within several million either way. Credible research calls for more than a well-meaning enquirer with a rain-soaked clipboard, asking a harassed housewife what she thought about *War and Peace*, whilst the dinner burns and baby falls out of her highchair. To obtain such results in depth would call for an army of researchers knocking on thousands of doors daily.

Perhaps, after several decades, we shall begin to learn the effects of an unbroken flow of programmes on an audience relatively captive in its home; an audience ranging in age from five to ninety, devouring anything from a situation comedy to a verse play from the Middle Ages, newly discovered in a remote Polish monastery. Then perhaps we shall begin to know what effect it has all had on us; and perhaps we won't like it very much.

I can judge only by my own years in drama. I would question whether anyone has ever had his way of life or convictions radically altered by what he saw in a drama. We may be pleased, saddened, angered or inspired by a play; our emotions may be moved by performances or delighted by the directors' or writers' sheer craft. But for how long do we stay touched? Does not real life take over again quickly? It is hard to believe that a wife, returning home from a play about a notorious poisoner, puts arsenic in her husband's cocoa; unless, of course, she has had it in mind for some time.

In 1907, the first performance in Dublin of J. M. Synge's *The Playboy of the Western World* ended in a public riot, a fierce moral protest against the play, one of whose characters was a loose-living village girl. In the late thirties, I walked on in a beautifully written play about Oscar Wilde; officially banned, it had to be produced in a club theatre, not because of any steamy content (there was none) but because Wilde was a homosexual. Neither play would raise an eyebrow today, nor do I believe they did any harm in their time.

Judging the potential sexual offensiveness of a script is a lot more difficult than assessing its violence. One steps into a minefield of contradictions, for what is sexually acceptable to one is obscenity to another. Nudity is deeply offensive to some; others are left cold by it, including, I imagine, the unclothed artistes. But can one write a legal guide on the subject – *The Producer's Handbook of Corporeal Exposure*? There is beautiful nudity, gross nudity, boring and unnecessary nudity. To show an ostensibly naked couple in bed (and how do so many television fornications prosper, when the man is wearing a coloured pair of briefs?) plainly enjoying a moment of post-coital bliss cannot offend me. I have less sympathy for the heaving gymnastics that were once the starting point of every new play, with Victor making Angela happy in a stoutly-built bed, accompanied by a sound track consisting of 'Oh, oh, Victor', and 'Ah, ah, Angela'.

There are thousands of broadminded viewers who still believe that the sexual act is special, and not for casual display. The intelligent playwright might consider whether his explicit scene is all that essential to the script. Audiences are quite capable of appreciating that a couple have just 'done it', without a demonstration of spring shattering dimensions. After all, most of us have had the pleasure.

Sexual scenes embarrass in different circumstances. A husband and wife will not blench at an explicit bedroom scene; but the same couple, accompanied by mother-in-law and twelve-year-old daughter, may be embarrassed. No harm will come to the experienced mother-in-law or the goggle-eyed offspring, but the master of the house may still switch off; and then the director has lost his battle. I can remember my own concern that young children should not gather an impression that sex was something giggly and furtive, or, from some of the more violent wedding night scenes, positively painful and joyless.

But what rules can one make? No Sex before Seven, no Nudity before Nine, no Eroticism before Eleven? Cut and dried pronouncements on public morality have always depressed me, if only because they are a direct invitation to evade them.

We are back to taste and common sense. Sexual content added to a dull script to give it spurious excitement cannot seriously be acceptable; it must grow naturally from the story. If there has to be a rule it is simple enough: if in doubt, in the special circumstances of television, don't do it.

In fact, I believe that violence and sex have been well controlled in television drama in this country, by which I mean domestically produced drama, for I have strong reservations about much of the bought-in feature films. There is a chain of responsibility in the majority of television managements that covers most controversies.

If this fails from time to time, through misjudgement or carelessness or sheer bad luck, we should not condemn the system, for the incidence of failure is small enough.

Complaints about bad language are more insistent and more frequent. In an age when four-letter words hardly raise an eyebrow, a spate of even the milder ones on television generates a gale of angry protests; sometimes due to a fastidious abhorrence of the words themselves, which are ugly, sometimes through embarrassment at hearing them in the company of family and friends. There is no doubt about the sincerity of such complaints. People react sharply to bad language, particularly when there is a lot of it. One 'shit' may pass, one 'piss-off' be tolerated. But if the script insistently rams the words home, the viewers first become irritated, and then angry. It is practically always an unnecessary alienation of the public. I can think of only one occasion when an extreme four-letter word was necessary to a play – the BBC's version of Trevor Griffith's *The Comedians*; and I had a hard fight to get that one agreed.

It is a simplistic argument to say that soldiers and sailors swear continuously, and that any play in barrack room or messdeck must maintain a steady stream of obscenities. I experienced all this in my five wartime years with the Royal Navy, but I see no profit in reproducing it in television drama. If the script is any good it will stand up without a false fortification of four-letter phrases.

Top of the protest list, perhaps surprisingly in a nation of ill-attended churches, comes blasphemy. If a character in a play persists in saying 'For Christ's sake', then as sure as God made non-blasphemous apples, there will be a crop of complaints the next day.

Public moralities change. Boundaries pushed out by one generation are pulled back by the next. I have no liking for mealy-mouthed pedantries. Let dramatists be bold and call a spade a spade. But the point can usually be made without calling it a four-letter shovel.

Television is incessant; if we choose, it can absorb most of our leisure time. It is not illogical that an unending flow of violence, sex and even four-letter words, can blunt the viewer's sensibilities by the insistent process of erosion, making him so familiar with cruelty and obscenity that he eventually accepts them as the norm. I have always distrusted the Scandinavian theory that if you soak people with continuous pornography, they will sicken of it and become sidesmen at the local Baptist chapel – an over-optimistic policy I would not wish to see tried in television. If the cure for violence is months of close shots of men being burnt and disembowelled, then we have indeed lost the fight. Such a diet of horror might have precisely the opposite effect. Instead of bringing the guinea-pig viewer to the point of revulsion, it might so deaden his sensitivity that anything, however horrible, would become acceptable.

There are occasional demands for a television censor, whose judgement would be a universal cure for all the ills of the medium; in truth it would need to be a small army of censors. The national turnover of drama alone would demand scores of men and women full time to cope with the flow; to which would have to be added the output of light entertainment, documentaries, features, even passages from books – everything of a fictional nature in television or radio. All would have to come under the general scrutiny. Nor would the censor go unchallenged. Each adverse decision would be passionately contested. It is difficult to keep up the flow of television drama; with such additional restrictions, the entire broadcasting system would seize up in a matter of months.

Only self-censorship will serve: a tightrope that programme makers must walk with resolution. It works well enough, and there are 'references above' and courts of appeal when things go awry. If the director is undecided, he has a producer. If they cannot agree, they have a head of department. Beyond them are controllers and managing directors, though appeal to them should be a last resort. The decisions of drama should stay in drama hands, and reference outside is an admission of failure – an invitation to future interference.

Drama is a public art, and is meaningless without an audience. Television has given it the largest audience in theatrical history. It is a gift that the makers of drama cannot accept without responsibility.

12

What Next?

'What next' is probably a question more technical than artistic. In three decades television has covered every facet of drama, from the fine to the fatuous. Drama – especially young drama – is always eager to abandon old ways for new images, and the rapid turnover of television accelerates the process. TV drama virtually started from scratch in the early fifties, but it came of age in record time.

It is the presentation of drama that changes continually. The content is more stubborn. *Titus Andronicus* in jeans and tracksuits is still *Titus Andronicus* though perhaps less credible than the original. Who was it said, at the end of this blood-soaked play, when the stage is littered with severed arms and legs, that they shouldn't have lowered the curtain, they should have drawn stumps?

There are pertinent questions for the future. 'How much television drama will there be in twenty years?' 'What sort and quality will it be?' and, probably most relevant – 'Who will be making it?'

That there will be more television generally in Britain is inevitable. The second ITV channel is about to open, and extra channels will be added by Cable/Subscription Television, and by satellite. Home recordings will flourish, with a brisk trade in cassettes and, later perhaps, videodiscs. Breakfast television is upon us, and no doubt, after that elevenses TV which, linked by afternoon transmissions to the evenings, will ensure there is no break in the bombardment.

Nor can breakfast television be confined to one channel only; the BBC and ITV will compete as vigorously for the early hours, as for peak viewing times.

In *The Listener* (12 November 1981) Alasdair Milne, then Managing Director of BBC Television, put the matter in a sentence: 'If the BBC is not actually involved in the early morning, there will come a time when, in news terms, people will turn to the other side;

they will naturally progress from the morning, through the middle of the day, and the evening.'

Which neatly encapsulates the recurring nightmare of the television impresario; once lost, a viewing audience is hard to entice back.

The next few years could see as many as five thousand hours of transmission added to the national output every year, the bulk of which would come from the fourth channel. It will be a major, perhaps unbalancing, factor. The new channel is owned by the Independent Broadcasting Authority, and part-funded by subscriptions – levies – from the ITV companies.

It is not intended that it be an equivalent of BBC2, or compete radically with ITV1 or BBC1. Its brief is to be different, to innovate and experiment. Its status will be that of the television 'publisher'. All but a small percentage of BBC and ITV television programmes are made 'in house', using the organisations' studios, equipment and servicing staffs. The fourth channel will not make its own programmes – it will draw them from ITV, from ITN and, most importantly, from independent programme makers; in doing so they are following a system long established in European television, where countries and organisations not only share productions and cost, but buy in a lot of independently made work.

How the fourth channel is bringing this about – and paying for it – we can consider in a minute. Meanwhile, what will this five thousand new hours of television have to offer drama?

Will there be a new production explosion, as there was in the fifties and the early sixties, when new series, serials, soap operas and play strands doubled the drama output? The seventies saw an abrupt levelling off, the new decade has, so far, threatened a decrease.

In 1952 the *seven hours* of Bernard Shaw's *Back to Methuselah* had a BBC budget of £3400, and a Francis Durbridge thriller serial £400 per thirty-minute episode. Five years later (1957) a ninety-minute production of O'Casey's *Juno and the Paycock* cost £1300, and the new Durbridge, though doubled in cost, was still a bargain at £800. Five years on again (1962) David Mercer's *A Suitable Case for Treatment* cost roughly the same as a fifty-minute episode of *Z Cars* – £3000. Another five years (1967) Jim Allen's full-length play *The Lump* cost only £14,022, more or less the going price for *The Wednesday Play*.

By 1972, with colour television established, a fifty-minute *Softly, Softly* was up to £24,000; Tom Clarke's *Stocker's Copper*, an all-film *Play for Today*, was £55,000, and a part-film, part-studio play

– *The Reporters* – was £37,000.

The figures for the seventies cannot give a mathematically accurate comparison, as they are based on an entirely different costing system. But the bizarre cheapness of the early dramas cannot be denied. Twenty years ago, writers, actors and directors were hardly over-paid; materials were cheaper, and production costs low, as practically all drama was transmitted 'live'.

But in those two decades (1952 to 1972) the rises in cost were at least logical and controlled, bearing no relation to costs today, only ten years later. In 1981/2 the budget for any drama-series or single play which was part film, part studio, was round about the £100,000 mark; an all-film series was almost £150,000, an all-film play was over £200,000. A major project like *The Borgias*, or a ninety-minute *Play for Today* film, would not leave much change out of a quarter of a million pounds at BBC rates, and considerably more elsewhere. To managements already on overdrafts, this may seem a high price to pay for a programme that will only have a life of two or three domestic transmissions, plus any profit from overseas sales.

Ironically, whilst popular series like *Secret Army* or *All Creatures Great and Small*, serials like *Brideshead Revisited* and *The Borgias* and *Tinker, Tailor, Soldier, Spy* attract large outside investment, and sell briskly round the world, the work of our best television play-wrights, like Dennis Potter, Jim Allen, Trevor Griffiths or the late David Mercer guarantees neither co-finance nor subsequent sales. Because they are *plays*, and the popular world market does not favour the single play. The battle to maintain a good volume of high-quality television drama is never completely won. Television moguls, competing mathematically for audiences (on which their careers may depend) are unlikely to go into raptures about a new production of *Peer Gynt*, or the latest Jim Allen political play.

Money is the key. There is no longer any cheap television drama. There is expensive, very expensive, and 'My God, you must be joking!' The simplest soap opera, using the same sets every week, a minimum of film, and a cast cut to below the level of credibility, still consumes a small fortune each week.

Yet a wide range of drama under the roof of one organisation is something to be prized and defended. It gives the schedules backbone and health. It allows producers to be bold, to experiment, and, occasionally, to fail.

If money is the key, it is not enough on its own to turn the lock. The *will* to sponsor the minority work must also be there. Television schedulers must bite on the bullet and accept that not every drama will top the audience ratings; that the sometimes depressing graph between quality and viewer millions is not, like so many other television statistics, to be regarded as an object of worship. Talent and enthusiasm are as nothing, if there is no platform for their creations.

Drama makers themselves have seen the dangers, and taken steps to put their overdrawn house into order. There have been streamlinings and cuts-down to the financial bone. But one can lean back to please too far. There is an artistic point of no return beyond which economy turns into idiocy; into the alternative of low quality or reasonable budget.

'Why not cheaper plays?' venture the financial moguls. By which, of course, they mean plays with two characters, one set and no filming. Difficult to convince them that a play with only two or three characters is the hardest to write, and an entire schedule of them would be a non-starter. If it were that easy, we would all be writing two-handers for the theatre, and making comfortable fortunes.

'Less scenery then?' insists authority.

Early television drama suffered from claustrophobia; sets had to fit into tiny studios. An early list of sets for a play would read: an ante-room in the Palace, a corner in the Kremlin, a corridor in the Old Bailey. Perfectly acceptable then; we were not, as we were later, trying to compete visually with the opulent and realistic conventions of the cinema. But today's list would read: The Throne Room in the Palace, the Council Chamber in the Kremlin, Number One Court at the Old Bailey; with a short scene in the House of Lords by way of linking them. But a return to the scenic modesty of early television would look shabby and second-rate, and would be fiercely resisted.

What is truly depressing is that an erosion of quality television drama, provided it were gradual enough, would probably not even be noticed by the majority of the viewing public. There would be no storm of protest about the absence of *St Joan*, or *The Three Sisters*, even *The Spongers* or *The Naked Civil Servant*. There are so many other diversions ... But that is a despairing argument. If, as it threatens, television becomes a social drug, then people might just as well be given the best quality powders.

TV drama has come of age. The new generation of writers and directors have not joined it from another medium – the theatre, films or journalism. Television is their first profession, and they have, understandably, no automatic regard for the old disciplines of production; disciplines made essential by 'live' transmissions. They have grown up with the medium and its technologies – it is no miracle to them. It is a tool, to be used to express and expand their ideas. They are looking for the dramatic realities, the documentary-type play, with all the fluidities of the cinema. They want to make pot-stirring, authority-challenging, social and political dramas on film – drama's most expensive ingredients – at a time when even the most modest budgets are under pressure.

If this determination to concentrate drama on location, film or video, were taken to its logical end, the vast electronic studios would become white elephants – unless they were given a new range of operation. I believe that managements and unions have to reach agreement to make all studios dual-purpose, for film or video recording, manned by crews who can work in either mode. There are signs that this will eventually come about.

Meanwhile, writers and directors must seek new and exciting ways of making drama in studios, or at least part-film, part-studio. Tape post-production is now as sophisticated as for film, and there is no reason for any director to feel that working in a studio is technically second best. The ideal remains obvious: let those who work best on film be given film; those who prefer tape-on-location be allowed that; and those who flourish in studios be given them. A liberal policy that is apt to come unstuck when everyone expresses an unyielding preference for film.

No major theatre play is paid for from one source. The cost is spread amongst a bevy of optimistic investors. Television drama has travelled cautiously down this road. It is fifteen years since I negotiated the BBC's first modest drama co-productions; not, in fact, co-productions at all, but co-financings, pre-investments to secure transmissions of our productions in the investor's area.

Co-production proper is a very different matter. It is a sharing not only of cash, but of talent, staff and resources – the script and producer from one partner, the leading lady and director from another; design and costumes from one, location resources from the other. Common practice in Europe, but few BBC drama productions have been of this pattern.

Whatever the nature of the partnership, the important factor is the artistic control. Drama is fragile enough, without subjecting it to the eroding interference of investors. Right or wrong, one man, or one woman, must be in charge, and ultimately responsible. Early BBC co-productions were very modest – our investors were getting an absurd bargain. But had they contributed a larger percentage of the total cost, it might have been harder to retain artistic control, and to maintain the impudent philosophy: 'Just give us the money, and leave us alone. We'll send you a print by and by . . .'

The bulk of the early co-productions was done with the United States, where the Public Broadcasting System (a string of stations across the major cities of America) was hungry for a television drama different from the usual ware on their screens.

PBS was set up, and part funded, by Congress in the sixties to provide a television and radio network that would enhance American broadcasting, as a contrast to the three highly competitive national networks, ABC, CBS and NBC, whose bitter competition has never allowed much room for minority programmes – difficult plays, the arts, documentaries. With them, ratings are all, and the result is an almost unbroken diet of chat-shows, quizzes, old films and news coverage in every form – punctuated by commercial breaks of a rare banality. Drama on these networks is mostly soap opera and series, made with great expertise and polished to a gloss and glitter particularly American. To be fair, there are occasional efforts to do something better. There has been a rash of blockbusting 'mini-series', inspired, I think, by the success of the British imports: opulent series like *Roots*, *Holocaust*, and the most excellent *Washington Behind Closed Doors*.

Public Broadcasting has the will to provide a richer diet, but not the weapons. Its financing is precariously dependent on Federal, State and local funding, donations from foundations, businesses and colleages – even auctions. They found it impossible to make enough quality programmes to fill their newly-won screens. American costs, then and now, make their British counterpart look like New Year sales in Oxford Street. The BBC, and later ITV, were on hand to supply precisely the sort of drama they needed – costume serials, adaptations from the great classics; modern adaptations like *Poldark* and *Penmarric*; family fare from Dickens and Stevenson and the great children's writers; and, later, new period series like *The Duchess of Duke Street* and *Upstairs Downstairs*; stories with rich and royal backgrounds like *The Pallisers*, *Edward VII* and *Lillie*.

This bonanza actually began in the last of the monochrome days with that staggering television success of all time – *The Forsyte Saga* – a serial that became part of British life.

Nor was PBS, in those booming seventies, the only American market. The old-established Hollywood giants like Warner Brothers,

Universal and Twentieth Century-Fox beat a path to the BBC Television Centre, lest they miss the British bus. For ludicrously low investments, they obtained the top quality television drama they were not themselves geared to make.

The American market is still there, but it is less eager, more particular. The buyers have realised that British television drama output is vast – they can afford to pick and choose a bit more. PBS, and the growing demands of cable television, may still create a demand, but the three networks continue to display their solid triptych of indifference; though blockbuster dramas like *Churchill and the Generals*, *Suez*, and *Burgess, Philby and Maclean* still raise a flicker of interest. American broadcasters have a respect for size. The great American novel is frequently just that – great, and heavy to hold on long air trips.

Sadly, much of our best television drama is neither the stunning blockbuster, nor the popular series. It is the new plays, written at their natural lengths of sixty, seventy-five or ninety minutes, indigenous in subject, locally accented, and uncompromising – the very qualities that work against them in this particular market.

We must accept the fact that there is little chance of regular succour for the single play from the States, on paper the most logical source, for the Americans speak (roughly) the same language as us, and there is no need for sub-titles. Play investment stands a better chance in Europe, and over the decade of the seventies I did co-productions with the French (a sticky wicket as they are still fretting about Waterloo); with the Dutch, who do good drama and share our sense of humour; with Belgium, Greece, Cyprus, Rumania and Yugoslavia, whose mounted troops came in most useful for *War and Peace*. There have been very fruitful co-operations with Australia, but all my efforts at co-operation with Canada were stillborn; which is curious, when one remembers how many fine directors that country lost to British television – Charles Jarrot, Ted Kotcheff, Silvio Narizzano, to say nothing of the legendary Sydney Newman.

Co-production is here to stay, but on different terms. The original idea was that the cash be used for enrichment – better casts, more filming, finer costumes. Today, for the more lavish productions, the investment has become essential. Serials like *The Borgias* do not cost tens or hundreds of thousands, they cost millions, and it is doubtful if such opulent projects will ever again be financed from one domestic 'in house' purse. How many companies could underwrite another *Brideshead Revisited*, without massive outside investment?

Happily such rich projects can still attract world interest. It is the single play that remains the Cinderella of TV drama, without the last dramatic satisfaction of a financial prince coming to the rescue.

As co-finance becomes more indispensable, the threat to the independence of the producer increases; once an outside investment reaches 40 per cent or more, it becomes harder to insist on artistic control. The final line of defence is sheer impudence: 'I know that you have generously contributed nearly 50 per cent of the budget, but I still insist on total artistic control of the script, casting and direction. I do not wish to discuss the matter further.' Anyone who can make that stick, deserves to win. The dangers of committee control are acute, particularly with casting. Everyone wants to cast, and if you are not careful you end up with an American Lord Nelson and a German Lady Hamilton. How well one remembers that boring period in post-war British films, when every picture had to star a European female starlet. This resulted in some exquisitely pretty actresses, with enchantingly cute accents, but it played hell with the credibility of the scripts; and it must have been very depressing for the young British starlets.

An alternative to foreign finance is to share the cost, domestically, with an independent producer. Such an arrangement was made for *Telford's Change* – the popular serial about banking – between the BBC and producer Mark Shivas, writer Brian Clark and actor Peter Barkworth. They supplied themselves, and scripts ready in every way for production. The BBC serviced the project, rehearsed and recorded it; in this sense, it was a true co-production, a sharing of talents and resources.

Independence is the new Mecca, getting away from the 'sausage machine' of the establishment, from being one of a hundred other projects, creating a freedom that maintains from first inspiration to final dub. A new spirit that should surprise no one. It is precisely what happened in the world of feature films, when many producers, actors and writers, tired of the paternalism of the great production houses, broke away to make their own films round the world – an action I well understand. As a television director I was never happier than when I escaped from the base and got out and about with a camera, a small crew and a handful of actors.

Whether the new independence poses a threat to the established centres of television production is another matter. Peter Jay, Chairman of TVAM (a breakfast television company), in his MacTaggart Lecture at the Edinburgh festival (Sept. 1981) was in no doubt at all:

We are well and truly in sight of a world in which significant parts of electronic publishing can both legally and practically take place, without coming within the existing purview of the broadcasting regulators. Video – both in tape and disc manifestations – is already the most highly developed form of this new wave. Cable, satellites (especially direct broadcast satellite services) teletext and other innovations are all contributing to what, from the cosy perspective of the closed circle of the authorised broadcasters, is regarded as the fragmentation of the audience. Even moderate developments such as the fourth channel, the Welsh fourth channel and breakfast television, which involve no technological innovation whatever ... are seen in some circles as threatening because they let newcomers, new ideas and new languages into the business: and even, more simply, because they might cause the existing stock of jam to be spread yet more thinly ... Quite simply, we are within less than two decades technologically of a world in which there will be no technical pretext for a government appointment policeman to allocate the air waves at all.

Jay went on to suggest that, by the end of the century, every household in the country would be able to watch as many different programmes as readers can read different books, magazines, newspapers, etc.

Later in the lecture, however, he conceded that:

The BBC and ITV would presumably continue as major 'publishers' on the new scene. But the Independent Broadcasting Authority would disappear, and the BBC would cease to be an authority with self-regulating powers and duties, as Broadcasting House can at present be said to exercise over the rest of the BBC ...

Strong stuff, and not to everyone's taste. Peter Fiddick, at the Royal Television Society's 1981 Cambridge Convention, whilst agreeing that the public might well be in favour of an end to institutional broadcasting, suggested that political attitudes might be less flexible.

'Politicians,' he added, 'will never be happy to let go that which they hold. They can do nothing about satellites and video. But the broadcasters will be very much in their grip.'

At the same convention, Paul Fox of Yorkshire Television expressed a 'healthy scepticism', wondering where the enemies of institutional broadcasting – the Cable and Pay TV entrepreneurs – were going to get enough programmes for their needs; and how long the paying viewer would enjoy being his own programme controller.

'How many times can you play *Gone With The Wind*? he demanded rhetorically. 'And how much will the man in Barnsley pay to see it?'

But beyond doubt we are entering a golden age of opportunity for the independent producer. There will be no shortage of drama ideas. But many independents will have limited finance and to remain in business will have to choose scripts and projects with a good chance of popular acceptance and sales potential; to achieve which may mean compromise. Many of them will have worked for long periods in the BBC or ITV, experiencing high artistic and technical standards, and will be loath to compromise for the sake of acceptance.

If this dilemma is their Dragon, then the fourth channel may be their St George.

Happily, Channel Four has for its chief executive a man of taste and courage – Jeremy Isaacs, whose plans for drama are firm and bold. Out of an initial programme budget of over one million pounds, from January 1982 to March 1983, he has committed a good portion to quality fictional work, much of which will be drama. He aims at fifty full-length all-film plays a year, plus soap operas and serials. He is adamant that at least 20 per cent of his programmes shall come from independent sources, as opposed to those which will come to him from the ITV companies. His strong public bids for the best talents may have helped to trigger off Paul Fox's reaction at the Edinburgh Festival:

'. . . the independents, the pay TV boys and those who make programmes for Channel Four, will cream off the attractive, the superficial and the headline-making, leaving the programme companies with the tough and difficult . . .'

An exaggerated fear, perhaps. But though Britain is rich in directors and writers, the best of them will undoubtedly go where the best attractions lie. Offer them something special and they find it hard to say 'No'. Yet, details and philosophies aside, one cheerful fact emerges – the new channel will open up a hundred new drama hours for the writer, the actor and the director.

There are no gold-paved roads in drama; if there are profits to be made in television, even the most popular-seeming series will not guarantee them. The great British institutional theatres – the National, the Royal Shakespeare, the best of the regional repertories – cannot survive without Arts Council backing, even if they play to capacity audiences every performance. In the commercial theatre, the impresario can lose the profits of three successes on one failure (the trick being, as it has always been in the theatre, to lose other people's money). The independent television impresario has his own problems. He must find money to secure writers and directors, to buy options of best-selling novels or successful plays; to attract talents to his side which will, in turn, make his production attractive. For if he is to begin at all, someone must want his project, invest in it, ensure its recording and transmission; beyond which extra profits must be sought on the international market, to which there is no easy road.

Television drama, even in the secure and serene days of BBC monopoly, has always benefited from its rebels – its Tony Garnetts and Dennis Potters, its Kenith Trodds and Jim Allens, whose comments and opinions are as hard-hitting and as irreverent as their productions. Television needs independent minds, and in the coming years must be generous to them; if it turns aside from those spirited enough to take the freelance road, it may be abandoning tomorrow's talents.

Cable and satellites, cassettes and videodiscs, are at the centre of any discussion about the industry's future. In the United States television by cable is a national reality, encouraged by the nature of the sprawling country, and the poor quality of its direct television signals – VHF rather than UHF; a situation fertile for the growth of multiple programmes by satellite and cable. The choice to the American viewer is both wide and narrow: wide in the sense that he can receive scores of channels, narrow in that many of them will offer him the same basic fare.

Ninety-nine per cent of the United Kingdom is covered by direct broadcasting on good UHF signals; which has undoubtedly helped to make the first cable experiments patchy and tentative. Today (summer 1982) there are experiments covering a dozen towns and areas, with more proposed. As a service it will increase, but it is questionable whether it will radically replace direct broadcasting before the end of the century, if then; beyond which date, any prediction must be suspect.

Cassettes, and the machines to play them on, will get cheaper and become a flourishing market in the future. But, by most expert technical opinion, the videodisc will take longer to establish itself.

What of regional television? – an ingredient to add spice to any television seminar. A degree of regionalism has existed for years, through the ITV companies, and the regional centres of the BBC. The brief of the BBC Drama Department in Birmingham was precise – to be regional. But it was a brief that covered every corner of

England except London, and as such could not be considered as truly and narrowly local.

At the Edinburgh Festival, Sir Dennis Foreman, of Granada TV, made the interesting point that a region served by the ITV system was simply an area covered by a common transmitter. Modern Britain, he felt, with its cultures based not on geography but on class and occupational strata, made the term 'region' something of a misnomer. 'The truth,' he added, 'is that the cultures of Toxteth, Brixton, Moss Side, Handsworth and Chapeltown have more in common with each other than the regionally related, more gentlemanly, towns of Chester, Guildford, Leamington Spa and Harrogate.'

Sir Dennis insisted that the viewers did not want that type of regional programming (the common transmitter area) – they wanted programmes about their village, their town, even part of their town. A view not universally shared by television impresarios; and one not very relevant to the drama maker; television drama is too costly to be made for local minorities.

There seems even less agreement about the future of broadcasting by direct satellite (DBS) in the United Kingdom. In the Home Office Study published in May 1981, Home Secretary William Whitelaw said:

> There was disagreement amongst those who submitted comments to the Home Office about whether, and if so when, the United Kingdom should embark on a Direct Broadcasting System. This is not surprising. No other country has experience of an operational DBS system, though some, notably France and West Germany, with their Government-backed projects, are actively preparing for or exploring this possibility. It is not therefore possible to make confident judgements about how direct broadcasting by satellite would operate in practice, whether viewers would be prepared to install the equipment needed to receive satellite broadcasts in their homes, or the extent to which the organisations concerned would wish to commit themselves to such a major investment for many years ahead.

He added later:

> We are prepared to give serious consideration to the option for as early a start as possible with satellite broadcasting, with perhaps one or two television channels, and possibly other information services . . . .

A pronouncement rich in 'possiblys' and 'probablys'. At a recent Conference held in Vienna on Satellite Broadcasting, Colin Shaw,

Director of Television at the Independent Broadcasting Authority, was also cautious:

> We need to ask ourselves whether satellite broadcasting is simply a variation of forms familiar to us over many years, or whether it brings in new elements which would radically alter our thinking and which perhaps call for fresh minds, inhibited by traditional ways of thought, or unhampered by obligations incurred over the years of conflicting interests . . . .

A statesmanlike way of suggesting a special committee to deal with the problems of satellites.

Colin Shaw stressed the necessity of restoring confidence amongst programme makers, management and investors after the ITV franchise reallocations; to concentrate on securing quality on ITV, of sustaining Channel Four in its first year of operations, of establishing breakfast television on a sound foundation. He added:

> I wait to be convinced that, at a time when people are showing signs of wishing to draw back from the mass, from the large scale, of seeking the local and domestic in preference to the international and grandiose, that satellites can sufficiently narrow their range to reflect at least this element in the contemporary mood . . . .

And later, in his speech:

> I could not regard as a great leap forward the introduction of a hundred channels, if it were accompanied by a contraction in the range of programming now available . . . .

I have sensed a like caution amongst many television experts and controllers: a feeling that there is already a lot to be done, in a country and a community unsettled by economic unrest: an instinctive reaction, perhaps of 'First things first.' No doubt Satellite broadcasting will arrive in good time, but I have not sensed an overridingly urgent demand for it amongst the practical programme makers.

'What Next?' as I said at the beginning of this chapter, seems a question more technical than artistic. I have my own apprehensions about the future of television drama – about that part of it, that is, that gains the smallest audience for the highest cost – the single play, the lesser-known classic.

The pattern of American-type television drama – an almost unbroken stream of glossy triviality – is depressingly successful, making the pleas for small-audience drama illogical to the mathematical mind. But we have something in this country worth preserving – a long drama tradition, begun in the theatre, continued in film, richly present in television, which has grown from a respect for the dramatic text, and a regard for its audience. If this professional concern is eroded in Britain (still the model for television drama) it could diminish everywhere.

The future means more hours of television, and a wider choice of channels; and hopefully, more drama. There are those who wonder if there will be enough talent to fill the extra hours, who fear that the existing talents are already spread too thin. I believe that we should discard these fears; we are rich in playwrights and dramatic invention.

Less certain is how long managements will continue to allocate large sums to the best of drama, without the return of the big viewing audiences. If programmes are wanted enough, the money is usually found. But if the pursuit of audience size and the blacking of the opponents' eyes becomes the main goal, then *all* standards, not just those of drama, must drop.

The ideal national broadcasting balance of audience is a rough fifty/fifty between BBC and ITV. Let one draw too far ahead of the other – to, say, a seventy/thirty situation – then the reaction of the other must be robust and commercial, to the detriment of minority programmes. Today this delicate balance maintains between the two, but the effect of Channel Four on the figures has yet to be felt.

In the affluent sixties, and early seventies, television drama blossomed under an expanding sky, and there was little difficulty in getting expensive minority programmes accepted into the schedules. Today, when costs have rocketed and money is short, it takes a steady resolution to maintain the flow. There are plenty of people in television drama who will fight to preserve the standards; but they cannot do it without hard cash, and the support of management.

Drama is a private world, resentful of outside intrusions. Its lively behaviour is often misconstrued by authority, who find its notions extravagant and its priorities incomprehensible. I sometimes suspect that there is a hint of envy behind these accusations, a feeling that drama people are getting something extra out of life, which is not fair.

Does television drama do us good? Is it a benefit, like electricity, anaesthetics, hot water and telephones? Television has become as important to daily life as these necessities; it is, too often, the automatic substitute for hobbies, conversation and the social graces. Certainly we have gained from it educationally, it has broadened our vision of the world's arts and customs, its fictions have delighted us. It has also compressed our leisure time, troglodyte fashion, into darkened rooms, so that we curse our neighbours if they dare to call, our friends and families if they tiresomely telephone. Is television to become an abundant Arcady, in which we are all to gambol as willing sheep?

If we are confident of our own resistance as mature adults, what of our children? Are we not in danger of creating a world for them in which television is assumed to be the prime diversion, approved by adults, and therefore blessed for children?

Perhaps in time this tide will reach a sort of full-moon height, and begin to subside in the face of some other universal attraction. The drama maker cannot stem it. He can only go on fighting for the money and talents to make his part of television as fine as possible.

No one should underestimate the power of television; nor overestimate its true importance, either. It is a tool, a service to something that is infinitely more important – life itself.

Picture credits
The publishers wish to thank the following for their kind permission to use copyright photographic material: The British Broadcasting Corporation, 1, 2, 3, 4, 5, 6, 7, 8, 9, 10, 11, 12, 13, 14, 15, 16, 17, 18, 19, 21, 22, 23, 24, 25, 26, 27, 28, 29, 30, 31, 33, 34, 36, 37, 38, 39, 40, 41, 42, 44, 45, 46, 47, 48, 49: London Weekend Television, 20: Thames Television, 32: Granada Television, 35, 43.

Index

ABC Television 18, 21, 83, 144
Abide With Me 28
actors, actresses casting 69–73, 146;
  and directors 13, 65–6, 108,
  112–15; in series 32
administration 18, 53
agents, theatrical 71–3
Age of Reason, The 36
Alice 18
Alice Through the Looking Glass 77
All Creatures Great and Small 21, 45,
  65, 80, 141
Allen, Jim plays 50, 54, 56, 89–90;
  production costs 140–1; rebel 149
All Good Men 28
All's Well That Ends Well 77
American television 21, 83, 144
Angels 34, 63–5, 69
Anna Karenina 63, 110
Antony and Cleopatra 77
Armchair Theatre 18
Attenborough, David 134
audience, of television 133–5
audience ratings 21, 23
audience research 134
auditions 70–1
Austen, Jane 35–6

Back to Methuselah 140
Barkworth, Peter 98, 146
Bar Mitzvah Boy 28
Barr, Robert 16, 31
Barrie, J. M. 24, 56
Bates, H. E. 38
BBC1, BBC2 18, 51, 140
BBC Drama Group 24
BBC Television Centre 17
BBC Television Drama 51, 53

Bennett, Arnold 36
Bennett, Rodney 101
Bergman, Ingmar 20, 54
Big Flame, The 20, 89
Billy 20
Bird, Maria 79
Birkin, Andrew 24, 56
Black Black Oil, The 20, 89
Blake's Seven 17
blasphemy 132, 137
Blooming Youth 89
Blue Remembered Hills 20, 90
Borgias, The 58, 83, 141, 145
Bowen, John 20, 28, 54
breakfast television 139, 151
Brideshead Revisited 141, 145
Broken Horseshoe, The 40
Brontës, the 35–7
Brothers, The 47
Browning Version, The 63
Burgess, Philby and Maclean 26, 145

Cable TV 147, 149
Calder, Gilchrist 25
cameras, TV 9, 91, 103–4
Candide 77
Caretaker, The 63
Cargill, Patrick 67, 108
Casanova 24, 39, 58, 83
casting 65, 69–73, 146
Cathy Come Home 18, 20, 25, 58, 89
CBS 21, 83, 144
censorship 138
Changeling, The 28
Channel Four (ITV2) 98, 139, 148,
  151–2
Cheviot, The 20, 89
children's drama 42–3, 89

Christ Recrucified 36
Churchill and the Generals 26, 57,
    145
Churchill, Winston 26, 57
cinema 30, 41, 60, 88, 122
Cinema 58
Civilisation 134
Clark, Brian 28, 98, 147
Clark, Kenneth 134
Clarke, Tom 16, 20, 28, 89, 140
classic adaptations 35–9, 62–3
Cold Comfort Farm 36
Colditz 62
Collins, Wilkie 40
colour separation 77
colour television 35, 140
Comedians, The 58, 137
commercial television 16
Common, The 28
Compact 46
Conroy, David 36, 58
Cooper, Giles 16, 31, 40
co-productions 143–5
Coronation Street 46–7, 69
costs of production 50–2, 99, 104,
    109, 120, 152; American 144;
    examples 140–1
costume designer 81–4
costumes 81–4, 113
Country Party, The 28
crime series 41
Crime and Punishment 39, 101
Crucible, The 63
current affairs programmes 129
Curteis, Ian 54, 57, 77

Daleks 44
Darlow, Michael 101
Days of Hope 90
Delderfield, R. F. 38–9, 45
design 73–80, 107
Detective 41
detective mystery 40–1
Devil's Crown, The 76–7
Diary of a Nobody 57
Dick Barton 40
Dickens, Charles 35, 40, 42
Direct Broadcasting System (DBS) 150
director role of 13, 65–9, 73–4, 78;
    background of 16; on location 90–8;
    at rehearsals 105–13; in studio
    117–20, 125–6
Diss, Eileen 78–9

Dixon of Dock Green 33
Doctor Finlay's Casebook 31
documentaries 25, 130
Douglas, Colin 67
Dracula 54
drama, history of 7–8; on television
    11–12, 15, 37, 74, 76, 109–11;
    future of 139–53
drama documentaries 24–6
Dr Jekyll and Mr Hyde 54, 86
Dr Who 19, 44, 77
dubbing 12, 121–6
Duchess of Duke Street, The 80, 144
Duchess of Malfi 28
Dunn, Nell 18, 89
Durbridge, Francis 40–1, 140

Ealing studios 88
editing 98, 122, 125
Edna the Inebriate Woman 20, 89
Edward and Mrs Simpson 39
Edward the Seventh 39, 83, 144
Eliot, George 36
Elizabeth R 20, 24, 39
Elliot, John 16, 31
endings of plays 28
Entertainer, The 63
Equity 19
Evacuees, The 28, 90
Evans, Dame Edith 36
Evita 76, 107
Eyeless in Gaza 36, 55
Eyre, Richard 58
84 Charing Cross Road 20

facility fee 94
Fair Stood the Wind for France 38
family sagas 39
Farnon, Robert 65
feature films 88–9, 109, 146
Festival 17
Fiddick, Peter 147
Fight Against Slavery, The 26, 134
film industry, British 8, 88
filming 12, 23, 38, 88–97
film schedule 94
film stock 122–3
First Churchills, The 39, 83
First Night 17
Fishing Party, The 28
Flint 56
Flying Swan, The 46
Ford, John 28, 50, 99

Foreman, Sir Dennis 150
Forsyte Saga, The 35, 39, 83, 144
For Tea on Sunday 17
Fox, Paul 147

Gambler, The 36
Garnett, Tony 25, 58, 99, 101–2, 149
General's Day, The 28
George and Margaret 53
Ghost Sonata, The 77
glamour 27
Glenister, John 9, 101
Glittering Prizes, The 20
Golden Bowl, The 55
Golden Vision, The 89
Gorge, The 20, 28, 89
Granada TV 46–7, 58
Grange Hill 43
graphic design 64–5
Graves, Robert 36, 38
Greene, Graham 36
Griffith, D. W. 121
Griffiths, Trevor 20, 28, 56, 58, 137,
   141
Grove Family, The 46

Hall, Willis 17, 54
Hamlet 44, 63, 101, 106, 120
Hard Labour 89
Hare, David 20, 90
Heads of Plays, BBC TV 53
Hearts and Flowers 20
Heidi 43
Henry VI 63
Henry VIII 39
Hollywood 27, 50–1, 83, 90, 94–5,
   109
Holocaust 144
Hopcraft, Arthur 20, 54
Hopkins, John 17–18, 20, 24, 31, 36,
   54
Horace 28
Horror of Darkness 18
Horseman Riding By, A 39, 45
Huckleberry Finn 89
Huxley, Aldous 36, 55

Ibsen, Henrik 7, 19
I, Claudius 36, 38, 63, 85
Imperial Palace 36
Independent Television 46, 49, 140
In Two Minds 25, 58, 89
Iron in the Soul 36

Isaacs, Jeremy 148
ITV2 (Channel Four) 98, 139, 148,
   151–2

Jacobi, Derek 85
Jane Eyre 83
Jarrott, Charles 89, 145
Jay, Peter 146–7
Jeapes, Alan 64–5
Jennie 83–4
Joe's Ark 20
Joffe, Roland 99
Jones, James Cellan 36, 55–6
Journal of Bridget Hitler, The 77
Juliet Bravo 69
Juno and the Paycock 140
Just a Boy's Game 90
Just Another Saturday 20, 90

Katy 43
Kidnapped 43
Kine, Jack 86
King Lear 77, 134
Kisses at Fifty 20, 89
kitchen sink genre 27
Kneale, Nigel 20, 54

Langrishe Go Down 56
Law and Order 20, 25, 56, 90
Le Carré, John 38
Leeds United 20, 89
Leigh, Mike 28, 89
length of plays 23–4
Let's Murder Vivaldi 20, 89
Letts, Barry 67
Licence Fee, BBC 56
Licking Hitler 20, 89
Lie, The 20
Life on Earth 134
lighting 114–18
Lillie Langtry 39, 83, 144
Lime Grove studio 89
Lingstrom, Freda 79
Listener, The 139
Little Minister, The 103
Little Princess, A 43
Little Women 43
live drama 9, 114, 119
Loach, Kenneth 89
locations 12, 88–102
Logan, Campbell 19
London Assurance, The 103
Lost Boys, The 24, 56, 101

Love Girl and the Innocent, The 103
Lump, The 89, 140

MacDonald, Graeme 57
McDougall, Peter 20, 90
McGrath, John 20, 31, 89
Mackenzie, Compton 36
MacTaggart Lecture 146
Mad Jack 20, 28, 89
Maigret 31
make-up 84–5
'man hours' 79
Marigold 7
Matthews, A. E. 110–11
Matthews, Francis 67
Mayor of Casterbridge, The 58
Mercer, David 17, 20, 54, 56, 89,
    140–1
Merchant of Venice, The 77
Messina, Cedric 55
Midsummer Night's Dream, A 103
Mill on the Floss 84
Miller, Arthur 63
Miller, Jonathan 77
Milne, Alasdair 139
Minder 63
Minton, Roy 28, 54
Mitchum, Robert 94–5
modern novel 38–9
Moonstone, The 40
Morahan, Christopher 54–5, 89
Morris, Colin 25
Mottram, R. H. 36
music 65

Naked Civil Servant, The 26
Nancy Astor 39
NBC 21, 83, 144
Nelligan, Kate 97
Newcomers, The 31, 46–7
Newman, G. F. 20, 25, 90
Newman, Sydney 17–19, 145
Nicholas Nickleby 84, 107
Nichols, Peter 16, 20, 28, 54, 89
Nigel Barton 18
nudity 135–6
Nuts in May 28

Oedipus Rex 19
Offers Meeting 54
Oliver 76, 107
Olivier auditorium 8
Olivier, Sir Laurence 37

Onedin Line, The 34, 61, 64
On Giant's Shoulders 26, 58
On The Eve of Publication 20, 89
Operation Diplomat 40
Osborne, John 54, 63
Owen, Alun 17–18, 54

pace, of play 98, 112
Pallisers, The 63, 83, 144
Parade's End 24
Paul Temple 40
pay TV 147
PBS (Public Broadcasting Service) 21,
    83, 144–5
Penmarric 39, 144
Pennies from Heaven 24
Peter Pan 56
Phillips, Leslie 72
Pinter, Harold 56, 63
*Playboy of the Western World,
    The* 135
Play for Today 18, 20, 25, 27, 58–9,
    89; costs of 140–1
Playhouse 17
Play of the Month 56
plays origins 15, 30; single 23, 27–9,
    52–62, 70, 89, 141–51; classic 62–3
Plays Department, BBC 17
playwrights 15–16, 21–3, 61
Poe, Edgar Allan 40
Point Counter Point 36
Poldark 144
police 41, 93
political reportage 128–9
Portrait Of A Lady 36, 55
post-production 121–7
post-war years 8, 9
Potter, Dennis 18, 20, 24, 28, 54, 59,
    90, 141, 149
Powell, Jonathan 58
Première series 24, 55
Prince Regent 39, 82–4
producer role of 49–60, 64–5; and
    director 67–70, 117
production assistant 115–18, 126
productivity 99, 104
Professional Foul 28
properties 111
property buyer 80
Prynne, William 29
Pulman, Jack 36, 63

Quantel 77

quartets 24–5
Quatermass and the Pit 86
Question of Honour, A 103
Quincey 77

Rattigan, Sir Terence 63
Raven, Simon 63
Rebecca 38
recording 119–20
Recruiting Officer, The 103
regional television 149
rehearsals 94, 105–15
'rehearse-record' 119
repertory theatre 108
Reporters, The 20, 141
Reprieve, The 36
Richard III 15
Roads to Freedom, The 36, 55
Robin Redbreast 20, 28
Romeo and Juliet 8
Roots 114
Rose, David 61
Rosenthal, Jack 20, 28, 56, 90
'rushes' 97–9

Sanderson, Joan 67
Sandford, Jeremy 18, 20, 54, 89
Sartre, Jean Paul 36, 55
satellites 149–51
Saturday Party, The 28
Saville, Philip 77
Savory, Gerald 16, 53–4
science fiction 44–5
Scott, Walter 43
script editor 23, 60–2, 68
scripts supply of 21–2, 57, 64; editing
　60–2, 67–8; reading and rehearsals
　107–9
Script Unit, BBC 21
Sea, The 56
Search for the Nile, The 26
Second World War 8
Secret Army 34, 64, 80, 141
serials 15, 18–19, 23, 35–40
Serials Drama Department, BBC 36
series 15, 23, 27, 30–4, 41, 63
series-al 34
set designer 73–81, 118
sets 73–80, 107, 142
sex 132, 135–7
Shakespeare, William 7–8, 15, 29, 55,
　63, 67, 77
Shaw, Colin 151

Shaw, George Bernard 7, 19, 140
Sherlock Holmes 40–1
Shivas, Mark 58, 98, 146
Shoestring 63, 90
Shooting the Chandelier 20
Shubik, Irene 58, 89
Sinister Street 36
six-part plays 24
Six Wives of Henry VIII, The 17, 20,
　24, 58
Soap 45
soap opera 11, 17, 27, 45–7
Softly, Softly 140
Spanish Farm, The 36
Speed King 26
Spend Spend Spend 20, 26, 56
Spongers, The 20, 25, 56, 90
Stag, The 20, 89
Star Wars 44
Stevenson, Robert Louis 43
Stocker's Copper 20, 28, 89, 140
Stoppard, Tom 28
Story to Frighten the Children, A 20
strand titles 17–18, 36, 42, 49–52,
　59–60
Stratford or Bust 28
Studio Four 17
studio space 12
studio time 116
Suez 26, 57, 101, 145
Suitable Case for Treatment, A 17,
　140
Suspense 17
Sutton, Shaun 18
swearing 132, 137
Sweeney, The 90
Sweeney Todd 76, 107
Sword of Honour 24
Synge, J. M. 135

Talking to a Stranger 20, 24
Tamburlaine 63
tape editing 12, 124–6
tape recording 99–104, 123
Target 90
Telford's Change 58, 98, 146
Testament of Youth 58
theatre-going 28
theatre plays 28–9, 49
Theatre Six Two Five 18
Thérèse Raquin 58
thrillers 40–1
Through the Night 20, 28, 56

Time Code 125
Tinker, Tailor, Soldier, Spy 38, 58, 64, 90, 141
'Tis Pity She's a Whore 28, 99
Titus Andronicus 8, 67, 139
Tom Brown's Schooldays 42
To Serve Them All Our Days 39
Traitor 28
Treasure Island 43, 88
Trevor, William 28
trilogies 24
Trodd, Kenith 58, 89, 149
Trollope, Anthony 35, 63
Troughton, Patrick 89
Turner, David 17, 36
Two Gentlemen of Verona 67

Underground Murder Mystery, The 8
United 46–7
Unloved, The 25
Upstairs, Downstairs 144
Up The Junction 18, 58, 89

Vanity Fair 36
video cassettes 72, 140, 149
videodiscs 139, 147, 149
violence 41, 132, 136–7
vision mixer 117
visual effects 86

Vote Vote Vote for Nigel Barton 58
Voyage of Charles Darwin, The 26, 134

War and Peace 23, 37, 63, 83, 92, 145
Warner, Jack 33
Washington Behind Closed Doors 144
Watford, Gwendoline 67
Waugh, Evelyn 24, 36
Wednesday Play, The 18, 20, 27, 58, 89, 140
Welland, Colin 20, 54, 89
Wessex Tales, The 20
When the Boat Comes In 34, 45
Where Adam Stood 28
Where the Difference Begins 17
Who Me? 25
Wilde, Oscar 7, 135
Wilkie, Bernard 86
William Brown 43
Williams, Keith 56
Wilson, Donald 18, 40
Woman in White, The 40
Wurzel Gummidge 43
Wuthering Heights 37, 84, 110

Year of the Sex Olympics, The 20

Z Cars 31, 33, 61, 140